ELI PELI • OPORTO FOODING HOUSE & WINE • JONATHAN'S

57 DINING & DRINKS • RIPE CUISINE • CHEF RONNIE KILLEN

IAN HOTEL, SPA & RESORT • CHEF HAROLD'S

BRASSERIE 19 • RAINBOW LODGE • MALAYA

DES CAFÉ • CIAO BELLO/TONY'S • GRACE'S

PALM • MAIN KITCHEN 806 LOUNGE AT THE DOWNTOWN JW

ONGKRAN THAI KITCHEN/GRILL • LOCAL FOODS • OXHEART

RUGGLES GREEN • IZAKAYA • FOREIGN CORRESPONDENTS

AKS COUNTRY CLUB • STATE OF GRACE • ARTHUR AVE

UDSON • QUATTRO, FOUR SEASONS HOTEL • BCN TASTE &

OL • JODYCAKES • DESSERT GALLERY & CAFÉ • DEER LAKE

A SEAFOOD CULTURE • PELI PELI • OPORTO FOODING HOUSE

D & WINE BAR • TABLE 57 DINING & DRINKS • RIPE CUISINE

R HOUSE, THE HOUSTONIAN HOTEL, SPA & RESORT • CHEF

CAFE ANNIE • RITUAL • BRASSERIE 19 • RAINBOW LODGE

IGINAL CARRABBA'S • ANDES CAFÉ • CIAO BELLO/TONY'S

PPERCLUB & BAR • THE PALM • MAIN KITCHEN 806 LOUNGE

CHEN & OYSTERETTE • SONGKRAN THAI KITCHEN/GRILL •

É • BORGO FOOD STATION • RUGGLES GREEN • IZAKAYA •

GATION • ROOST • RIVER OAKS COUNTRY CLUB • STATE OF

D Y VINO • HUBBELL & HUDSON • QUATTRO, FOUR SEASONS

NA ITALIANA • CARACOL • JODYCAKES • DESSERT GALLERY

SONESTA HOTEL • PESKA SEAFOOD CULTURE • PELI PELI

ADA CUISINE • IBIZA FOOD & WINE BAR • TABLE 57 DINING &

AX AMERICANA • MANOR HOUSE, THE HOUSTONIAN HOTEL,

EF ERIN SMITH FEGES • CAFE ANNIE • RITUAL • BRASSERIE

FOOD & WINE • THE ORIGINAL CARRABBA'S • ANDES CAFÉ •

ACK • PROHIBITION SUPPERCLUB & BAR • THE PALM • MAIN

DOG • LIBERTY KITCHEN & OYSTERETTE • SONGKRAN THAI

• HUNGRY'S CAFÉ • BORGO FOOD STATION WINE • CHEF A

HOUSTON
SOUPS & SIPS

HOUSTON
SOUPS & SIPS

ERIN M. HICKS
WITH JODIE EISENHARDT

Soup's on!

CaptiView

Houston, Texas

The word "Captiview" and the Captiview logo are trademarks of Captiview, Inc., and are registered in the U.S. Patent and Trademark Office.

U.S. Patent and Trademark Office

ISBN 978-0-9858776-9-9

Text by Erin M. Hicks, Jodie Jones Eisenhardt

Edited by Erin M. Hicks, Jodie Jones Eisenhardt, Diane Hause, Jennifer Howard

Photography by Erin M. Hicks, William Jones Miller, Debora Smail, David Skinner, Ellliot Tate

Artwork by Erin M . Hicks

Production by Erin M. Hicks

Based on a design by Erin M. Hicks

Printed in China

Published by Captiview, Inc.

Houston, Texas 77007

www.captiview.net

FOR OUR
GRANDMOTHERS -
AND YOUR
GRANDMOTHERS, TOO!

TABLE OF CONTENTS

INTRODUCTION

Historically speaking, soup is considered to be as old as cooking itself. When food was scarce, combining various ingredients into a pot to boil was cheap and filling, with each culture adopting its own variations based on whatever was available.

Historians believe soups like broth, bouillon and consommé made their debut in "restoratifs" (the word from which we derive "restaurant") in 18th century Paris. However, archeological discoveries of heatproof/waterproof pottery in China in 2013 suggest that tradition of making some form of soup goes back at least 25,000 years.

The word soup comes from French *soupe* ("soup", "broth"), which comes through the Latin *suppa* ("bread soaked in broth"), from a Germanic source, from which also comes the word "sop", a piece of bread used to soak up soup or a thick stew.

All we know is that everybody loves soup and we'd be really happy if more people were making it at home, feeling and sharing the love that soup creates. To that end, we offer up this tasty collection of chefs' recipes along with some advice on preparing them from the perspective of a home cook.

About Ingredients
We care about what all of us are eating – it's true! We absolutely believe how well your soup turns out has as much to do with the quality of ingredients, as it does with following the recipes we have obtained and tested from Houston's nest chefs. For us, that means using organic ingredients whenever possible. We also seek pastured/grass-fed meat, poultry and dairy along with wild-caught seafood. We are particularly against anything made with GMO-corn/corn syrup and we very much encourage purchasing ingredients from local farmers' markets, CSA farm shares and directly from farmers. There are so many great resources available now, locally and online! Read labels, educate yourself, and give thought to where your food comes from and what you really want to put into your body and those you care about. The more you learn and experience what comes out of your kitchen using clean ingredients, we promise you will feel as passionately about this as we do!

About Equipment
While you might not need more than a good stockpot for the basics of soup, we would like to point out the value of a Vitamix blender for creating extraordinary texture for the blended soups (never mind how much we love it for smoothies). You can get greats deal on the certified reconditioned models.

About Broth and Stocks
If you're in a pinch for time, go ahead and use packaged broth or stock. Again, use organic whenever possible. Keep in mind that you can make and freeze stock easily, and this helps you to always be soup-ready. A few basic stock and broth recipes are included in the back of the book, but also consider searching online for a wealth of recipes and resources.

About Process
You'll notice that for some of the recipes, we will offer the longer process based on the chef's recipe along with our shortcuts, so you can choose which way you'd rather go. Some days we feel more like short-order cooks than wanna-be chefs; we bet you feel the same. Having said that, there are few things more satisfying than following a long, detailed process (as we felt when we made our own lard for Prohibition's gumbo recipe) and relishing in the result. Try some things you've never attempted before – it's gratifying to get outside of your comfort zone every now and then.

**ONLY THE PURE OF HEART
CAN MAKE GOOD SOUP**

— LUDWIG VAN BEETHOVEN

GERMAN ROOT VEGETABLE
ARA, ROYAL SONESTA HOUSTON

This recipe is one of the finest vegetable soups - ever! It has German roots, just like Peter Laufer, the former executive chef of The Royal Sonesta's, globally-inspired Ara restaurant. The Galleria-area hotel recently enjoyed a massive, $25M renovation of the entire property resulting in gorgeous accommodations, along with showy public spaces, including the sophisticated Axis lounge.

YIELD: 12 SERVINGS

¼ cup	unsalted butter
½ tsp	garlic, diced
I cup	onion, diced
I cup	carrots, diced
I cup	parsnip, diced
I cup	celery root, diced
½ cup	turnip, diced
I Tbsp	marjoram, chopped
I Tbsp	oregano, chopped
I cup	russet potato, diced
I cup	parsley, chopped
10 cups	vegetable stock
2-3	bay leaves
I cup	leeks, diced
to taste	salt and pepper
3 Tbsp	chives, chopped, *for garnish*
	ground nutmeg, *for garnish*

Melt the butter in a large stockpot over medium heat, add the garlic and the onions, and sauté until translucent, about 10 to 15 minutes.

Add the carrots, parsnip, celery root and turnip, and sauté for 3 to 6 minutes.

Keep stirring, and add the marjoram and the oregano.

Add the potatoes, half of the chopped parsley, and the vegetable stock.

Bring to a boil, add 2 to 3 bay leaves, and a little salt and pepper.

Reduce the heat, add the leeks and simmer for 30 minutes, stirring frequently.

Set aside for 30 minutes, season to taste, with salt and pepper, and reheat again.

To serve:

Ladle the soup into bowls.

Finish with the remaining parsley and chives.

Sprinkle with nutmeg.

Wine: A bright, cherry-packed Sangiovese, like Chianti Classico
Beer: A sour stout, like Tart of Darkness, from The Bruery

ORGANIC PEA SOUP
PESKA SEAFOOD CULTURE

Young chef Omar Pereney is a TV super-star in Latin America. He has quite a flair for dishes with clean, fresh flavors utilizing stellar ingredients. No wonder we adore him and the superb Peska on Post Oak. They have a fantastic happy hour, Monday through Friday featuring Delamotte champagne (Erin's favorite!) for just $10 a glass!

Recipe Notes: Instructions to clarify butter are on page 131.

YIELD: 4 SERVINGS

Cut off the leek stems, remove the outer leaves, and cut off the dark green parts.

Soak the leeks in water to clean off any remaining dirt or sand.

First, julienne the leeks: cut them into long, thin strips, then turn and dice them into ⅛-inch cubes.

In a sauté pan on medium-low heat, add the butter and the leeks, and cook until they turn transparent, about 20 minutes.

Add the stock or water, and increase temperature to bring to a simmer, for about 15 minutes.

Add the peas, and cook for 3 minutes, on medium heat.

Blend the mixture, while adding the tarragon until very smooth.

Strain the mixture, and add salt and white pepper, to taste.

Cool down the soup as quickly as possible, if not serving right away.

Heat the stock in a saucepan, over medium-high heat.

Add the peas and cook for 4 to 5 minutes. Strain.

Heat the ghee in a skillet, over medium heat.

Add the poached peas, leeks, bacon bits and salt, and sauté for a few minutes.

To serve:

Add the sautéed pea mixture to warmed serving bowls in a semi-circle.

Garnish with the pea sprouts.

Add the hot pea soup to a pitcher and serve tableside.

4-5	leeks, trimmed, white part only
½ cup	unsalted butter
1 Tbsp	fresh tarragon
5 cups	vegetable stock or water
4 cups	organic peas
to taste	salt and white pepper
1½ cups	vegetable stock
2½ cups	organic peas
2 Tbsp	ghee (clarified butter)
¾ cup	leeks, white part only, small dice
¼ cup	bacon bits or crisp pancetta
1 tsp	salt
½ oz	pea sprouts, *for garnish*

Wine: A Grüner Veltliner
Beer: A traditional IPA, like Saint Arnold Elissa

CARROT GINGER
PELI PELI

Chef Paul Friedman, owner and executive chef of Peli Peli put the unique flavors of South African cuisine on the map in Houston. The restaurant has been featured on the Food Network and CNBC, and Chef Paul has also competed on Cutthroat Kitchen!

Recipe Notes: His Peli Peli seasoning is a traditional South African spice mix, available for purchase at their Galleria location. An all-purpose seasoning mix is a good substitute.

1 Tbsp	vegetable oil
1¼ lb	carrots, sliced
¾ cup	yellow onion, diced
½ Tbsp	garlic, chopped
10 cups	water
¼ cup	orange juice
1 Tbsp	chicken base
½ Tbsp	Peli Peli seasoning
¼ cup	brown sugar
1½ tsp	ground ginger
1¼ cups	heavy cream
	crème fraiche, *for garnish*
	Peli Peli seasoning, *for garnish*

YIELD: 6 SERVINGS

In a stockpot, heat the oil over medium heat.

Add the carrots, onion and garlic.

Sauté until translucent, 10 to 15 minutes.

Add the water, orange juice, chicken base, seasoning, brown sugar and ginger.

Bring to a boil, then reduce to a simmer.

Simmer for 30 to 45 minutes, until the carrots are tender, and the water is reduced.

Carefully add the mixture to a blender, and purée until smooth.

Return to the pot, then add the cream, and mix well.

To serve:

Ladle the soup into serving bowls.

Garnish with a little crème fraiche and a sprinkle of seasoning.

Wine: A South African Pinotage or a Steen (Chenin Blanc)
Beer: A pale lager, like Baltika 7

CALDO VERDE
OPORTO FOODING HOUSE & WINE

One of the most beautiful new restaurants in the city, this Midtown tapas hot spot is the sibling to the original Greenway Plaza location. This recipe from chef Rick Di Virgilio is for their famous Portuguese "green soup," hence the name.

Recipe Notes: You may substitute water for the chicken broth, for a vegetarian soup.

YIELD: 6 SERVINGS

¼ cup	extra-virgin olive oil
1 cup	white onion, medium dice
2	bay leaves
1 Tbsp	garlic, minced
1½ lb	Idaho potatoes, peeled, quartered
¼ tsp	white pepper
2 qt	chicken broth
½ Tbsp	salt
1 cup	kale, shredded
drizzle	Portuguese olive oil grilled chorizo, *for garnish*

Add the olive oil to a medium stockpot, over medium heat.

Add the onions and bay leaves, and sauté until translucent, about 10 minutes. (No color on the onions).

Add the garlic, and quickly sauté, about a minute.

Add the potatoes, white pepper and chicken broth.

Cook for 30 minutes, until the potatoes are fully cooked, and the broth has reduced.

Blend the soup until smooth, with an immersion blender, or in a regular blender.

Return the soup to the pot.

Add the salt, and continue to reduce the soup for another 10 to 15 minutes.

Add the kale, and allow to cook a few minutes longer.

To serve:

Ladle the soup into bowls.

Drizzle with Portuguese olive oil.

Serve with or without grilled chorizo.

Wine: A Portuguese Vinho Verde
Beer: A blonde ale, like El Boquerone

JALAPEÑO CHICKEN
JONATHAN'S THE RUB

This is an award-winning soup! It took first place last year at the annual Chicken Soup cook-off, at Congregation Emanuel. Chef Jonathan Levine is known for his mouth-watering burgers, his famous "Rub" seasoning and the restaurant serves our favorite coconut cream pie, in the city!

YIELD: 6 SERVINGS

2 Tbsp	olive oil or unsalted butter
4	poblano peppers, seeded, diced
2	yellow onions (medium), diced
4	red jalapeños, seeded, diced
pinch	salt and black pepper, freshly ground
1½ cups	chicken stock
1½ cups	heavy cream
1 cup	Monterey Jack cheese, shredded
1½ lb	chicken thighs, boneless, skinless
to taste	salt and black pepper, freshly ground
	cilantro leaves, *for garnish*
	red jalapeños, diced, *for garnish*

Heat the olive oil or butter over medium heat, in a large, heavy-bottomed stockpot.

Add the poblano peppers, onions, jalapeños, a pinch of salt and black pepper.

Sauté for approximately 10 minutes.

Reduce the heat to low, and add the stock, cream, cheese and chicken.

Cover and simmer, stirring occasionally, for 30 minutes, or until the chicken is cooked through.

Remove the chicken and shred.

Return the shredded chicken to the stockpot.

Season to taste, with salt and black pepper.

To serve:

Ladle the soup into serving bowls.

Garnish with cilantro leaves and red jalapeño.

Serve immediately.

Wine: A New Zealand Sauvignon Blanc
Beer: A German pale ale, like GPA, from 3 Nations Brewing Co.

GAZPACHO
BOADA CUISINE

Chef Arturo Boada is a Houston legend who spoils everyone at his namesake restaurant, just off of Voss road. The super-fresh seafood, pastas, salads, and more from the sparkling kitchen, makes us very happy.

Recipe Notes: Cholula is a Mexican hot sauce readily available at most grocery stores, or you can substitute your favorite hot sauce. A recipe for croutons is on page 41.

YIELD: 8 TO 12 SERVINGS

Combine all of the ingredients except for the garnishes in a large bowl and mix well.

Purée the mixture in batches in a blender.

Refrigerate for at least 30 minutes.

To serve:

Ladle the soup into bowls.

Garnish with croutons, red onion, red bell pepper, egg yolks, chives and egg whites, either on the side, or on top of the soup.

2 Tbsp	extra-virgin olive oil
1⅓ Tbsp	garlic, chopped
¼ cup	white vinegar
½ Tbsp	black pepper, finely ground
2¼ tsp	salt
1 lb	cucumber, peeled, diced
1 Tbsp	Cholula hot sauce
1 Tbsp	lime juice
2 cans	whole, peeled tomatoes (28-oz)
1½ cups	water
1 cup	soda water
	croutons, *for garnish*
	red onions, diced, *for garnish*
	red bell pepper, seeded, finely chopped, *for garnish*
	egg yolks, cooked, finely diced, *for garnish*
	chives, finely diced, *for garnish*
	egg white, finely diced, *for garnish*

Wine: A Sangiovese-Cabernet Sauvignon blend
Beer: A cream ale, like 8th Wonder Dome Faux-m

POTATO-LEEK-AVOCADO
IBIZA FOOD & WINE BAR

Obtaining this delicious recipe involved Erin receiving a $1000 bar tab for bubbles!

Ibiza remains one of our go-to restaurants. We're crazy for Chef Charles Clark's lovely Spanish cuisine and some of the best wine prices in the city. Erin swears that his Indian-chutney-glazed sea bass is one of the best seafood dishes she's ever eaten!

YIELD: 2 SERVINGS

I Tbsp	olive oil
I cup	Yukon gold potato, peeled, diced
I	garlic clove, minced
½ cup	celery, diced
I	leek, white and light green parts only, washed, thinly sliced
3 cups	chicken broth
I tsp	lemon juice
2 Tbsp	Greek yogurt
I	avocado, peeled, seeded, chopped
I	lemon, zest of
to taste	salt and pepper
2 tsp	Greek yogurt, *for garnish*
	avocado, cubed, *for garnish*
	parsley leaves, *for garnish*

Heat the olive oil in a small stockpot, over medium heat.

Add the potato and garlic, and cook for about 2 minutes, stirring occasionally.

Add the celery, leek, and I cup of the chicken broth, and simmer on low for 5 minutes.

Transfer the mixture to a blender.

Add the lemon juice, yogurt, I cup of the chicken broth and the avocado.

Purée for about 30 seconds, or until smooth.

Return the purée to the pan, and add the remaining cup of broth.

Heat until simmering, about 3 to 5 minutes, on medium heat.

Turn off the heat, and stir in the lemon zest.

Add salt and pepper, to taste.

Refrigerate until chilled.

To serve:

Divide the soup between two bowls.

Top with a teaspoon of yogurt, if desired, and garnish with cubed avocado and parsley leaves.

Serve cold.

Wine: A Vinho Verde, with a hint of effervescence
Beer: A saison, like Moody Tongue Steeped Emperor's Lemon Saison

SEAFOOD GUMBO
TABLE 57 DINING & DRINKS

Former Brennan's and Haven Chef, our friend Randy Evans' cuisine lives on at this genius idea of a great restaurant, within the gorgeous new HEB on Fountainview. Can we get a collective hallelujah on how fortunate we are to have HEB in Houston?

Recipe Notes: A seafood stock recipe appears on page 130 but you may purchase seafood stock boxed or refrigerated at most grocery stores. We utilized Airline Seafood's seafood stock, available locally, frozen by the quart. To minimize okra slime, combine 1 quart of water with 1 cup of cider or distilled vinegar, and let the sliced okra soak for an hour. Pat dry before cooking. You may substitute a pound of fish (cut into pieces) for a pound of the shrimp, or a combination of the seafood. Randy recommends using Emeril's "Essence" or Paul Prudhomme's "Seafood Magic" for the seasoning, but he also approved our use of Old Bay Seasoning to give a bit more of an east coast flavor profile vs. NOLA-style. Extra roux will keep in the refrigerator for several months.

YIELD: 6 SERVINGS

For the brown roux:

In a heavy 4- to 6-quart saucepan, add the oil over high heat, until it starts to smoke.

Add flour, ¼ cup at a time, letting it become a dark, nutty brown before the next addition. Be sure to stir continuously, so the flour doesn't burn.

When all of the flour has been added, and the mixture is a rich brown color (think chocolate), remove from the heat.

Stir in the remaining ingredients. This will start to cool down the roux, bring out more color, and add flavor. Transfer the roux to a bowl or container, and let cool down.

When cool, refrigerate until ready to use. Some of the oil will come to the top when chilled; mix it back in before using.

For the gumbo:

In a heavy saucepan, heat the oil and butter over high heat, until it starts to smoke.

Sauté the celery, bell pepper, onion, jalapeño, garlic, okra and tomato for 5 minutes, or until the okra is no longer slimy.

Combine the wine and spices with the sautéed vegetables, cook down until the wine is almost evaporated.

Stir in the stock, bring to a rolling boil and then add the roux.

Return to a boil, then simmer for 30 minutes.

Adjust the seasoning, if necessary. Stir in the seafood, and cook for 5 minutes more.

To serve:

Ladle the gumbo into warm bowls, over spoonfuls of rice.

Garnish with green onions and parsley leaves.

Wine: An old world Viognier
Beer: An IPA, like Deschutes Inversion IPA

BROWN ROUX

2 cups	vegetable oil
3 cups	all-purpose flour
⅓ cup	yellow onion, minced
⅓ cup	green bell pepper, seeded, minced
⅓ cup	celery, minced
1 tsp	garlic, minced

GUMBO

2 Tbsp	vegetable oil
2 Tbsp	unsalted butter
1 cup	celery, diced
1 cup	bell pepper (small), seeded, diced
2 cups	yellow onion (small), diced
½	jalapeño, minced
2	garlic cloves, minced
2 cups	okra, sliced
½ cup	tomato, diced
½ cup	white wine
½ tsp	cayenne pepper
½ cup	seafood seasoning
½ Tbsp	kosher salt
3 qt	seafood stock
2 cups	brown roux
1 cup	parsley, minced
1 pt	oysters
2 lb	Gulf shrimp (medium), peeled, deveined
1 lb	crab claw meat
5 cups	long grain rice, cooked green onions, minced, *for garnish* parsley leaves, *for garnish*

LUCK & PROSPERITY
RIPE CUISINE

Chef and dietician Stephanie Hoban has one of our very favorite food trucks in town. Her commitment to seasonal, organic cuisine inspires us to think more about what we're eating and where it comes from - with deliciously satisfying results!

YIELD: 6 SERVINGS

2 tsp	olive or grapeseed oil
1½ Tbsp	garlic (5-6 cloves), minced
1	jalapeño, seeded, minced
1	shallot (medium), minced
1	carrot (large), peeled, small dice
1 Tbsp	tomato paste
2	bay leaves
1 tsp	ground cumin
1 tsp	smoked paprika
¼ tsp	chipotle chili powder
¼ tsp	salt
1 can	fire-roasted tomatoes (14.5-oz)
6 cups	low sodium vegetable stock
1 Tbsp	maple syrup
1 cup	black-eyed peas, dried, soaked overnight
2 cups	cauliflower florets
1 cup	whole wheat or gluten-free pasta
½ lb	kale, stems removed, rough chopped
	green onions, sliced, *for garnish*

In a large pot over medium-high heat, sauté the garlic, jalapeño and shallot in oil, for 3 to 5 minutes.

Add the carrots, tomato paste, bay leaves, spices and salt.

Stir in the tomatoes, and sauté for 2 more minutes.

Add the vegetable stock, maple syrup and black-eyed peas.

Cover and increase the temperature to bring to a boil, about 20 minutes.

Once boiling, reduce the heat to medium-low, and simmer for 30 minutes, or until the black-eyed peas are tender.

Remove the bay leaves.

Add the cauliflower and the pasta, and cook until both are al dente, about 10 minutes.

Stir in the kale just prior to serving, to wilt.

To serve:

Ladle soup into bowls.

Garnish with green onions

Wine: A voluptuous, honeyed Viognier, from the northern Rhone valley
Beer: A cloudy, orange-spiced Belgian-style witbier, like Real Ale White

TURKEY CHILI
CHEF RONNIE KILLEN

Chef Ronnie Killen is known for his nationally lauded restaurants, serving up BBQ, steaks, and now even burgers. Truth be told, he's actually into healthy cooking as well. As we like to say, it's all about balance!

Recipe Notes: You can often find ancho chili powder in the spice section of the grocery store, but to make your own, simply seed and remove the membranes of about 4 to 5 ancho chiles. Heat the oven to 375°F and toast the chiles for about 10 minutes. Place the chiles in a spice or coffee grinder and process into a fine powder. This chili also makes for a great Frito Pie - just add some shredded cheese, a dollop of sour cream, and fresh or pickled jalapeños (a pickled jalapeño recipe may be found on page 62)! And, you can make this ahead of time: it can be refrigerated for up to 3 days.

YIELD: 6 TO 8 SERVINGS

In a saucepan, heat the oil over medium-high heat.

Add the turkey, season with salt and pepper, and cook over moderate heat, breaking up the meat, until white throughout, 4 to 6 minutes.

Add the garlic, onion, chile powders and the cumin and cook, stirring, until fragrant, 5 minutes.

Stir in the tomatoes, tomato sauce and the water, and bring to a simmer.

Cook over low heat, stirring occasionally, until thickened, about 45 minutes.

Add the beans, and simmer for 15 minutes.

Meanwhile, light a grill or heat a grill pan.

Grill the tortillas over moderate heat until soft, 30 seconds per side and wrap in a towel.

Season the chili with salt and pepper.

To serve:

Serve with the grilled tortillas.

Garnish with pickled or fresh jalapeños, if desired.

2 Tbsp	extra-virgin olive oil
1 lb	lean ground turkey, white meat only
½ tsp	salt
½ tsp	black pepper, freshly ground
3	garlic cloves, minced
1	onion (medium), finely chopped
2 Tbsp	ancho chile powder
1 Tbsp	New Mexico chile powder
1 tsp	ground cumin
1 can	tomatoes (14-oz)
1 can	tomato sauce (15-oz)
1 cup	water
1 can	black beans (15-oz), drained, rinsed
to taste	salt and pepper
	corn tortillas, grilled pickled or fresh jalapeños (optional), *for garnish*

Wine: A Barossa Valley GSM, exhibiting smoked meat, cherry, rhubarb and licorice notes

Beer: A German pilsner-style beer, like B-52 Payload Pils

Chef David Skinner from the charming restaurant Eculent in Kemah wanted to make a soup from an ingredient that lots of folks don't think they like - and blow their minds. Well done, chef, well done!

His aerated version of this soup is ethereal, for sure. The more simplistic version here is still divine and is in fact Erin's mother's favorite soup in the whole book!

YIELD: 6 TO 8 SERVINGS

CAULIFLOWER SOUP

1	white cauliflower head
3	garlic cloves, peeled
2 cups	whole milk
1½ cups	heavy cream
2 Tbsp	unsalted butter, softened
1 tsp	salt
½ tsp	white pepper

PARMESAN CRUMBLE

8 oz	Parmesan cheese, freshly grated, *for garnish*
	purple cauliflower, *for garnish*

For the cauliflower soup:

Heat the oven to 350°F.

Cut the cauliflower into flowerets, and place on a silpat (or parchment paper) on a sheet pan, along with the garlic cloves.

Place in the oven and bake until golden brown, usually 30 to 45 minutes, depending upon the oven.

Add the cauliflower and garlic to a blender, and purée with the milk.

Once the cauliflower is starting to turn into paste, slowly add the cream, and continue blending until smooth.

Add the butter, salt and pepper.

For the Parmesan crumble:

Heat the oven to 375°F.

Place the shredded cheese in a thin layer on a silpat (or parchment paper) on a sheet pan, and place in the oven for approximately 20 minutes.

Remove once the cheese has melted together and has a slight caramel color.

Do not let it turn brown as it will taste burnt.

Remove from the oven and let cool completely.

Once cool, crumble the cheese "cookie" using either a food processor or mortar and pestle.

To serve:

Ladle the soup into bowls or serving container of choice.

Garnish with thinly sliced freeze-dried, or fresh purple, or other colored-cauliflower (use a mandoline, if you have one) and the Parmesan crumble.

Wine: A Sauvignon Blanc or a Pinot Noir
Beer: A dry or sparkling cider, like Eric Bordelet Sidre Tendre

CELERY ROOT VELOUTE
PAX AMERICANA

What can we say about chef Adam Dorris and Pax Americana? Incredible ingredient sourcing with genius outcomes, like this scrumptious velvety soup that Jodie's mom really loved. Sommelier and owner Shepard Ross' wine list is one of the most thoughtfully curated lists in the city!

Recipe Notes: Look for Makrut lime leaves (also known as kafir lime leaves) at Asia Market or online. Fennel pollen is available at Central Market or online.

YIELD: 8 SERVINGS

Make a small sachet utilizing the cheese cloth, with thyme, bay, lime leaf, fennel seeds and black peppercorns.

In a large stockpot, add the olive oil over medium-low heat and sweat the celery root, celery, apple, potato, fennel, garlic, ginger and onion for 15 minutes, stirring often, to avoid caramelization.

Add the white wine and allow the alcohol to cook out for 5 minutes, over medium heat.

Add the sachet and cook with the other ingredients for 2 minutes.

Add the water and slow simmer for 1½ hours, over medium heat.

Add the coconut milk and the coconut cream, and allow to cook on low heat for 20 minutes.

Remove from the heat and strain the cooked vegetables, reserving all cooking liquid.

Transfer the cooked vegetables to blender at a ratio of 1:3 (vegetables to cooking liquid), and blend until smooth and creamy. Work in batches appropriate for blender size.

Pass through a fine mesh strainer.

After all has been blended, add any additional cooking liquid to the puréed mix, and incorporate with a whisk or immersion blender, until smooth.

Add the lemon juice, and season with kosher salt, to taste.

To serve:

To finish, either serve warm or chilled, add a few tablespoons of Greek yogurt to each bowl, with a spoonful of granola. Garnish with cilantro sprigs and shaved fennel.

Pour the soup around the garnish, dust with fennel pollen, and enjoy.

1½	thyme sprigs
2	bay leaves
1	Makrut lime leaf
2 Tbsp	toasted fennel seeds
2 Tbsp	black peppercorns
1	cheese cloth
¼ cup	extra-virgin olive oil
1	celery root head, small dice
1	celery stalk, thinly sliced
½	Granny Smith apple, peeled, cored, small dice
½	russett potato, peeled, small dice
½	fennel head, small dice
½	garlic clove, shaved thin
¼ cup	ginger root (4-inch), peeled, grated
½	onion (small), small dice
¼ cup	dry white wine
8 cups	water
1 cup	coconut milk
⅓ cup	coconut cream
2 Tbsp	lemon juice
to taste	kosher salt
1 cup	Greek yogurt
1 cup	savory granola
	cucumber slices, *for garnish*
	Asian pear slices, *for garnish*
	peach slices, *for garnish*
	fennel pollen, *for garnish*

Wine: A Melon de Bourgogne, from Loire Valley, with vibrant acidity and minerality
Beer: A balanced American IPA, like Community Beer Co. Mosaic IPA

FRENCH ONION
MANOR HOUSE, THE HOUSTONIAN HOTEL, CLUB & SPA

One of Houston's historic gems, the Manor House, previously known as The John Staub estate, once served as the home of George H.W. Bush while director of the CIA and vice president of the United States, and as the place where the G7 Economic Treaties were signed.

Recently open to the public after 30 years as a private dining space for hotel guests and Houstonian Club members, Executive chef Neal Cox and chef Roland Soza are putting out impeccable versions of classical dishes – with a twist, like this delightful French onion soup – all amidst flawless service.

YIELD: 6 SERVINGS

SOUP

4 Tbsp	olive oil or unsalted butter
6 cups	yellow onion, sliced
4 Tbsp	dry sherry
3 Tbsp	flour
6 cups	beef stock
to taste	salt and pepper

CROUTONS

1	brioche or baguette, cut into ½ to 1-inch cubes
1 Tbsp	unsalted butter, melted
12 oz	Gruyère cheese, grated
1 Tbsp	thyme leaves, chopped, *for garnish*

For the soup:

Heat a heavy, oven-safe stockpot, over medium-low heat. When the pot is hot, add the oil or butter. Stir in the sliced onions, ensuring they are evenly coated.

Cook the onions for 30 to 45 minutes, stirring every so often to make sure they aren't burning, until caramelized. The onions should be brown and very tender, once finished.

Increase the heat, and add the sherry to the pan. Cook down for a few minutes, until almost all the wine has evaporated.

Reduce the heat to medium-low and stir in the flour. Cook for 2 to 3 minutes, until the flour forms a thick paste (add a tablespoon of butter, if needed).

Add 1 cup of beef stock, and stir for a couple of seconds. Add the rest of the stock and bring to a boil, then reduce the heat and simmer for 30 minutes.

Season the soup to taste, with salt and pepper.

For the croutons:

Preheat oven to 325˚F.

Coat the bread with butter, and place on a baking sheet.

Toast the bread in the oven for 10 minutes, or until golden brown.

To serve:

Turn on your oven broiler.

Ladle the soup into heat-proof ramekins.

Place a few croutons into the soup, forming a single layer of bread. Sprinkle a thick layer of Gruyère cheese over the top.

Broil until the cheese bubbles and starts to brown. Remove the ramekins from the broiler with extreme caution.

Garnish with thyme leaves.

Wine: A French Burgundy or a Pinot Noir
Beer: An ale, like Buffalo Bayou Brewing Co. 1836 Copper Ale

WATERMELON GAZPACHO`
CHEF MARK COX

Mark's American Cuisine is no longer open, but Mark Cox will forever remain my favorite Houston chef. Jodie and I fell in love with this soup, the summer before he closed, and the recipe absolutely had to be included in this book. His delicious blueberry tart graced the cover of my very first book, "Houston Classic Desserts."

YIELD: 6 SERVINGS

For the soup:

In a 2-quart saucepan, over moderate heat, add the olive oil, garlic, lemongrass and shallots, stirring until the mixture is lightly golden.

Purée the watermelon in a blender until smooth and slowly stir into the shallot mixture. Bring to a boil and remove from the heat.

Carefully return the mixture to the blender. Add the lime juice and chile, and blend.

Taste, and adjust the seasoning, as necessary.

Pour mixture through a sieve or strainer into a bowl, and chill until ready to serve.

For the crab-mango salsa:

Pick through/clean the crab meat, removing any shells.

Peel and seed the mango, and cut into a fine dice.

In a mixing bowl, toss the crab, mango, cilantro and the watermelon.

Add the olive oil and lime juice, and season with salt and pepper.

Press the mixture into a 3-inch round cookie cutter or mold, and refrigerate until ready to serve.

For the tempura shrimp:

Heat the oil in a deep saucepan to 375˚F.

In a mixing bowl, add the club soda and stir in the rice flour.

Season the shrimp with salt and pepper, and dip into the tempura batter to lightly coat the shrimp (not too heavy on the batter).

Fry until golden brown.

To serve:

Add about half a cup of soup to small chilled bowls, place the crab-mango salsa on top, then finish with the shrimp and cilantro leaves.

WATERMELON SOUP

2 Tbsp	olive oil
1 Tbsp	garlic, minced
1	lemongrass stalk (5- to 6-inch), roots trimmed, outer stems discarded, minced
3 Tbsp	shallots, finely chopped
6 cups	watermelon, cubed, seeded
2 Tbsp	lime juice
1	Thai or Serrano chile (small), minced
to taste	salt and pepper

CRAB-MANGO SALSA

½ lb	jumbo lump crab meat
½	mango, ripe
¼ cup	cilantro, chopped
¼ cup	watermelon, finely diced
1 Tbsp	olive oil
1 Tbsp	lime juice
to taste	salt and pepper

TEMPURA SHRIMP

3 cups	vegetable oil, *for frying*
½ cup	club soda
½ cup	rice flour
6	wild-caught shrimp, peeled, deveined
	cilantro, flowering or leaves, *for garnish*

Wine: A Riesling, white Burgundy or Chablis
Beer: A Belgian witbier, like Blanche de Bruxelles

CREAM OF BROCCOLI
HAROLD'S TAP ROOM

Louisiana-accented fare by NOLA transplant Antoine Ware, who worked alongside James Beard Award-winning chef, Chris Shepherd at Hay Merchant, features excellent sourcing from local farmers and ranchers, which we totally appreciate!

Recipe Notes: Reserve some of the broccoli florets for garnish. A recipe for croutons is on page 41.

YIELD: 4 TO 6 SERVINGS

I Tbsp	olive oil
I	yellow onion (medium), diced
I	celery stalk, diced
2	garlic cloves, diced
I tsp	thyme leaves, chopped
8 cups	broccoli, stems and florets, chopped
6 cups	chicken broth, vegetable broth or water
½ cup	heavy cream
to taste	salt and black pepper, freshly ground
	broccoli florets, *for garnish*
	croutons, *for garnish*

Heat the oil in a stockpot, over medium heat.

Add the onion and the celery and cook, stirring occasionally until soft, 4 to 6 minutes.

Add the garlic and the thyme, and cook for about 20 seconds.

Stir in the broccoli, add the broth (or water), and bring to a boil over high heat.

Reduce the heat to a simmer, and cook until very tender, about 8 minutes.

Purée the soup, in batches in a blender, until smooth.

Return to the pan. Stir in the cream, and add salt and pepper, to taste.

To serve:

Ladle the soup into serving bowls.

Garnish with the reserved broccoli florets and croutons.

Wine:　An Austrian Grüner Veltliner
Beer:　An American lager, like The Crisp, from Sixpoint Brewery

BUTTERNUT SQUASH
CHEF ERIN SMITH FEGES

Chef Erin Smith Feges started making this recipe while she and her sister lived together in a tiny NYC apartment. They were broke and had no "real" kitchen, so their home-cooked meals required resourcefulness and no more that one pot, one burner, and a small cutting board. She was working at Babbo at the time and had access to the butternut squash scraps, which prompted the origins of this soup. It evolved over time into this scrumptious version.

Recipe Notes: Use any stale bread you have for the croutons!

YIELD: 6 SERVINGS

For the soup:

In a stockpot or Dutch oven over medium heat, sauté the onions and fennel in olive oil until translucent, approximately 5 minutes.

Sprinkle in the red chili flakes, and allow to toast for a minute.

Increase the temperature to high, and add the wine to deglaze the pan.

Let the wine come to a boil, and cook down for 5 minutes. It will reduce slightly, concentrating the flavor.

Add the cubed butternut squash, pour in the chicken stock, and continue to cook covered, until the squash is fork-tender, approximately 30 to 35 minutes.

Once the squash is cooked, remove the pot or Dutch oven from the heat. Purée, using a immersion blender, or pour into a blender in batches, and blend until smooth.

During this process, add salt and white pepper, until you reach your desired flavor.

For a restaurant quality-smooth soup, pass through a fine mesh sieve, lined with cheese cloth.

For the croutons:

Heat the oven to 325˚F.

Cube the bread and toss in the olive oil, salt, and pepper. Bake until golden brown.

To serve:

For the crème fraiche, add ¼ cup to a metal bowl, and whisk until it reaches soft peaks.

Ladle the soup into bowls.

Add a dollop of crème fraiche, and drop in a few croutons.

SOUP

1 cup	yellow onion, diced
1 cup	fennel bulbs, diced
½-1 Tbsp	red pepper, crushed
2 cups	white wine, preferably Riesling
3 lb	butternut squash, cubed
4 cups	chicken stock
to taste	salt and white pepper

CROUTONS

2	stale bread pieces, cubed
1 Tbsp	olive oil
to taste	salt and pepper
¼ cup	crème fraiche, *for garnish*
	parsley leaves, *for garnish*
	red pepper, crushed *for garnish*

Wine: A Riesling
Beer: A Belgian pale ale, like Orval Trappist Ale

WILD MUSHROOM
CAFE ANNIE

The iconic Cafe Annie is back! After taking on the name "RDG+Bar Annie" during the restaurant's big move in 2009, 2016 found chef Robert Del Grande celebrating 35 years in the kitchen, and a return to the original name. This soup reminds us of why his accolades include a James Beard Award - it's simply divine.

Recipe Notes: The duck prosciutto garnish should be cut into very thin slices - thin enough to easily curl. Oyster or crimini mushrooms may be substituted for the portobellos. A recipe for croutons is on page 41.

YIELD: 6 SERVINGS

4 Tbsp	unsalted butter
2 Tbsp	garlic cloves, peeled, chopped
¾ cup	yellow onion, peeled, chopped
4	California Mission figs, dried, stems removed, chopped
1	pasilla, ancho or chipotle chile, stemmed, seeded, rough chopped
8 oz	portobello mushrooms, stems removed and discarded, caps chopped
1 can	huitlacoche (7-oz)
2 cups	chicken stock
½ tsp	salt
½ tsp	black pepper
1 cup	heavy cream
	toasted brioche croutons, *for garnish*
	duck prosciutto, thinly sliced, *for garnish*

In a broad deep pot, heat the butter until foaming, over medium heat.

Add the garlic, onion, figs and dried chile, and sauté until golden brown, about 4 to 6 minutes.

Add the mushrooms, and sauté until the mushrooms are well cooked, about 4 to 5 minutes.

Add the huitlacoche, and continue to sauté until the mixture is a rich dark color, about 2 to 3 minutes.

Remove ¼ cup of the vegetable mixture, before adding the stock. Set aside.

Add the chicken stock, and simmer for approximately 30 minutes.

Remove from the heat, and allow to cool to room temperature.

Transfer the mixture, in batches if necessary, to a blender, and purée until smooth.

Add the salt, pepper and the cream.

Adjust the thickness of the soup with a little chicken stock or cream, if necessary.

Adjust the seasoning, to taste.

Blend the reserved vegetable mixture, until smooth. Set aside.

To serve:

Add the toasted brioche croutons, and a small quenelle (*football-shaped scoop*) of the vegetable mixture to serving bowls.

Place the duck prosciutto curls on top.

Gently pour the soup around the garnish, and serve.

Wine: An Austrian Zweigelt, with dark fruit, violet flowers and pepper
Beer: A dry Irish stout, like Rauchtabout, from Spindletap Brewery

SEAFOOD GRAVY
RITUAL

Ritual is a collaboration between Black Hills Meats' Felix Florez and restaurateur Ken Bridge. It was an instant success, featuring stellar ingredients, utilizing pastured meats and locally-sourced produce. We're enamored by a number of menu items, including the Angry Bird, the juicy burgers and salads that will make you smile really big - all with huge flavors! This gravy must be sopped with delectable, grilled bread.

Recipe Notes: A recipe for seafood stock appears on page 130. You may purchase seafood stock jarred, boxed or refrigerated, at many grocery stores. You may also purchase frozen stock at Airline Seafood.

YIELD: 8 TO 10 SERVINGS

For the gravy:

Melt the butter in a large stockpot, over medium heat.

Add the onions, garlic and salt, and cook until translucent, about 15 minutes.

Add the bell pepper and celery, and cook for another 10 minutes.

Add the tomato paste, and cook to slightly caramelize, for about 10 minutes.

Add the stock, heavy cream, anchovies, bay leaves, lemongrass, Worcestershire and paprika.

Bring to a boil, while whisking thoroughly. Boil for 10 minutes.

Add the rice, and simmer for 20 minutes, or until the rice is cooked.

Remove from the heat. Stir in the wine and the bourbon. Remove the lemongrass.

For the seafood:

Heat a large sauté pan until searing hot, add the grapeseed or olive oil, and turn until the pan is coated.

Lightly coat the snapper and shrimp, with kosher salt and cracked pepper

Place the snapper and shrimp in the pan for 3 minutes, without turning.

Then add the seafood stock, butter and crab, and stir for a few minutes.

To serve:

Ladle the gravy into bowls, and evenly distribute the seafood mixture amongst them.

Serve with grilled sourdough.

GRAVY

¼ cup	unsalted butter
2½ cups	onion, small dice
¼ cup	garlic, minced
1⅓ Tbsp	salt
2⅓ cups	red bell pepper, seeded, small dice
¾ cup	celery, small dice
6 Tbsp	tomato paste
5 cups	fish or seafood stock
5 cups	heavy cream
5	anchovy filets
4	bay leaves
⅓ oz	lemongrass, crushed
1 Tbsp	Worcestershire
1⅛ tsp	paprika
1⅓ cups	long grain rice
1⅛ cups	white wine
2 Tbsp	bourbon whiskey

SEAFOOD

½ cup	grapeseed or olive oil
8 oz	snapper, skin-on, cut into 1-oz slices
8 oz	Gulf shrimp, shelled, deveined, seared
to taste	kosher salt and cracked black pepper
1 cup	seafood stock
3 Tbsp	unsalted butter
8 oz	lump crab meat
	parsley leaves, minced, *for garnish*
	grilled sourdough

Wine: A rich, golden, full-bodied Roussanne, with ripe pear and toasted oak notes
Beer: A crisp blonde ale, with subtle orange peel and nutmeg, like Chimay Triple Blonde

Brasserie 19 remains the place to see and be seen, but one of the best kept secrets is this vividly fresh-tasting soup. The hint of mint makes it especially refreshing on a warm day.

Recipe Notes: Water may be substituted for the chicken stock but do not use broth. Dry-roasting the beets will give you the most flavor, however they can be oil-rubbed and wrapped with foil, "baked potato-style", for easy clean up. The beets can totally be roasted ahead of time!

5-7	red beets (small to medium)
1	English cucumber, peeled
½	sweet yellow onion (large), rough chopped
⅔ cup	white wine
1½ cups	Greek yogurt
2 Tbsp	lemon juice
1 qt	chicken stock
to taste	salt and pepper
	micro-mint leaves, *for garnish*

YIELD: 6 SERVINGS

Heat the oven to 500˚F.

Roast the beets with the skin on for 30 to 45 minutes.

Peel the beets when cool.

Cut the beets and the cucumber into pieces small enough for a blender.

Add the onion, wine, yogurt, lemon juice and stock to a blender, and purée until smooth.

Taste and adjust seasoning, with salt and pepper.

To serve:

Ladle the soup into serving bowls.

Garnish with mint.

Wine:　A bone-dry Loire Chenin Blanc
Beer:　A sour, German-style wheat beer, like Saint Arnold Boiler Room

MOROCCAN EGGPLANT
RAINBOW LODGE

Rainbow Lodge is one of our favorite places and the talented Mark Schmidt is a chef to be reckoned with. He served this delicious soup at a Lucky Dog fundraiser we had at Revival Market last year. We were immediately smitten with it and asked for the recipe right then and there.

Recipe Notes: Ras el Hanout is a Moroccan spice blend. It can be purchased locally at Phoenicia Market or Whole Foods. The duck stock recipe is on page 136 but chicken may be substituted. Pre-cooked duck confit may be purchased at Spec's and at Central Market.

YIELD: 6 SERVINGS

For the eggplant soup:

Preheat oven to 375°F.

Slice the eggplant in half lengthwise, and brush the cut side with all but 1 tablespoon of the olive oil. Season the eggplant with half of the Ras el Hanout, and place cut-side down, in a baking pan.

Roast in the oven until tender, about 30 minutes.

After eggplant is cooked and cool enough to handle, scrape the flesh from the skins, shred and reserve, discarding skins.

Heat the remaining olive oil in an large stockpot, over medium heat.

Add the onion, celery, garlic and jalapeño and cook until softened and just starting to color, about 10 to 15 minutes.

Add the thyme and the rest of the Ras el Hanout, and cook for another 5 minutes.

Add the duck (or chicken) stock and reserved cooked eggplant, bring to a boil, and lower to a simmer. Cook for 10 minutes.

Transfer the soup to a blender in batches, and purée, covering the blender top loosely with a kitchen towel. Be careful to allow steam to escape, while puréeing.

Season to taste, with salt and pepper.

To serve:

Add the duck confit to the middle of the soup bowls.

Pour the hot soup over the duck confit.

Garnish with Greek yogurt and parsley leaves.

EGGPLANT SOUP

4	eggplant
¼ cup	olive oil
1 Tbsp	Ras el Hanout
1 cup	onion, chopped
½ cup	celery, chopped
3	cloves garlic, crushed
1	jalapeño, seeded, chopped
1 tsp	thyme leaves, chopped
1 qt	duck stock
to taste	salt
to taste	pepper
1 cup	duck confit, pulled (about 2 legs), room temperature
2 Tbsp	Greek yogurt, *for garnish*
1 Tbsp	parsley, chopped, *for garnish*

Wine: An Alsatian Gewürztraminer, with luscious peach and caramel notes
Beer: A saison/farmhouse ale, like Saison Dupont

POBLANO
51FIFTEEN

The new 51-fifteen Cuisine & Cocktails, inside the new Saks Fifth Avenue is a spectacularly beautiful and sexy place, dressed in gray, white and black, with shiny gold accents, by local designer Nina Magon. We are huge fans of opening chef Stefon Rishel, who had just parted ways with the restaurant at press time. We can only hope that the fresh, seasonally-inspired and oh-so-flavorful dishes we've come to expect, like this luscious soup, will continue to live on.

Recipe Notes: Instructions for toasting pumpkin seeds are on page 131.

YIELD: 4 TO 6 SERVINGS

1½ Tbsp	extra-virgin olive oil
5	poblano peppers, seeded, rough chopped
½	Spanish onion (large), rough chopped
1	jalapeño, seeded, rough chopped
2	garlic cloves, chopped
2 qt	chicken stock
½	russet potato (large), peeled, rough chopped
½	cilantro bunch
to taste	salt and pepper
	pumpkin seeds, toasted, *for garnish*
	cilantro, *for garnish*
	sour cream, *for garnish*

In a large stockpot, heat the olive oil over medium-high heat.

Add the poblanos, onion, jalapeño and garlic.

Sauté until softened, about 15 minutes.

Add the chicken stock to deglaze the pot, and bring to a boil.

Add the potato, and cook for 45 minutes.

Turn off the heat, and add the cilantro.

Purée with an immersion blender, or in a traditional blender, until smooth.

Season to taste, with salt and pepper.

To serve:

Ladle into bowls.

Garnish with pumpkin seeds, cilantro and sour cream.

Wine: A dry Rosé or a sweet Picpoul
Beer: A Mexican-style beer or a nice, hoppy IPA, like Karbach Hopadillo

MULLIGATAWNY
HIMALAYA

Recently enjoyed by Anthony Bourdain, and named #10 on Alison Cook's 2016 "Top 100 Restaurants" list, chef Kaiser Lashkari's Himalaya is a beloved Houston institution. The name of this soup literally means Pepper Water. It's a classic Anglo-Indian creation, and a delightfully wholesome soup to be enjoyed by all.

Recipe Notes: Lal Masoor Dal is the preferred brand of red lentils. You can find tamarind concentrate/paste at most Asian markets, or you may substitute a tablespoon of tomato paste. Instructions to clarify butter are on page 131.

YIELD: 16 SERVINGS

½ Tbsp	ghee (clarified butter)
1 cup	onion, finely chopped
6	garlic cloves, minced
2½ tsp	ginger, grated
4	green chile peppers, chopped
¼ tsp	cinnamon
¼ tsp	cloves, ground
1½ tsp	coriander seeds, ground
2 tsp	cumin seeds, ground
1 tsp	turmeric powder
1 Tbsp	roasted Madras curry powder
1 Tbsp	fresh curry leaves, chopped
4	green cardamom pods, bruised
2	celery stalks, chopped
2	carrots (medium), cubed
1	apple (large), peeled, cored, chopped
1	potato (medium), peeled, diced
1	sweet potato (medium), peeled, diced
1¼ cups	red lentils
10 cups	chicken stock
2	lemons, juiced
3 cups	coconut milk
1½ tsp	tamarind concentrate, seedless
2	chicken breasts, boneless, skinless, boiled, cubed
4 oz	basmati rice, cooked
to taste	salt and black pepper
3 oz	sour cream or yogurt, *for garnish*
2 Tbsp	cilantro or flat leaf parsley, chopped, *for garnish*

Heat the ghee (clarified butter) in a large pot, over medium heat.

Add the onions, and while stirring continuously, add the garlic, ginger, chiles, cinnamon, cloves, coriander, cumin, turmeric, curry powder, curry leaves and cardamom pods.

Make sure to keep stirring, so nothing burns on the bottom of the pan.

Cook until the onions are lightly brown, and the mixture starts releasing aroma.

Add the celery, carrots, apple, potato, sweet potato, lentils and chicken stock to the pan.

Let simmer, uncovered, for 20 minutes, or until the vegetables and lentils are tender.

Remove the cardamom pods.

Transfer the soup in batches, to a blender, and purée.

Sieve the soup, and then return it to the pot.

Add the lemon juice, coconut milk, and tamarind to the pot, and heat the mixture, while stirring.

Add salt and pepper, to taste.

To serve:

Ladle the soup into a bowl or cup.

Add a spoonful of rice, boiled chicken, sour cream or yogurt, and cilantro or parsley, for garnish.

Wine: A big, juicy, oak-influenced Chardonnay
Beer: An American pale ale, like Karbach Weekend Warrior Pale Ale

AVGOLEMONO
HELEN GREEK FOOD & WINE

We're so fond of chef William Wright's simply wonderful, award-winning cuisine, enjoyed in the chic space Erin designed in Rice Village. Written up by the New York Times and a James Beard semifinalist in its first year, Wright utilizes immaculate ingredients to create dishes that celebrate the clean, vivid flavors of Greece. The dishes are perfectly paired by sommelier and Helen-visionary Evan Turner, who has crafted the second only all-Greek wine list in the country. It's not like anything else in the city and this soup says it all.

Recipe Notes: You may use turnip, collard, mustard, chard or beet greens. You may substitute ancho chile pepper for the Aleppo. A recipe for croutons is on page 41. Follow the cooking instructions on the orzo paackage.

YIELD: 4 TO 6 SERVINGS

SOUP

1 Tbsp	roasted garlic paste (about 7-8 cloves)
1 qt	chicken stock
1 tsp	salt
1 tsp	Aleppo pepper
1 cup	greens, chopped

AVGOLEMONO

2	eggs
½ cup	lemon juice, freshly squeezed
to taste	salt
1 cup	orzo, cooked
1 cup	artichoke hearts, jarred, drained
5 Tbsp	extra-virgin olive oil
¼ cup	dill sprigs, *for garnish*
1 cup	croutons, *for garnish*
3	scallions, thinly sliced, *for garnish*

For the soup:

Heat the oven to 375°F. Drizzle the garlic cloves with a little olive oil, and place in a foil packet. Roast until soft, about 30 minutes. Squeeze the garlic from the skins and mash with a fork, to make a paste.

In a medium-sized stockpot, bring the chicken stock to a simmer, over medium-high heat, for about 5 minutes. Whisk in the roasted garlic paste, and season the broth with salt and Aleppo pepper. Add the chopped greens, and cook for 5 minutes.

For the avgolemono:

Combine the eggs and lemon juice in a double boiler, over medium heat, and continuously whisk, until the mixture is thickened. (If you don't have a double boiler, simply combine the mixture in a bowl, that fits on top of a saucepan, filled about ⅓ full of water.) Season to taste, with salt.

Add the avgolemono to the soup, whilst vigorously stirring, so that it does not clump, over medium heat, for like 30 seconds.

Add the orzo and artichoke hearts. Simmer for another 5 minutes, and adjust seasoning, if necessary.

To serve:

Ladle into serving bowls.

Garnish with dill, croutons and scallions.

Wine: A naturally rich, fruity, dry, northern Greece Malagousia
Beer: A bright lager, like Greek FIX Lager

LENTIL
THE ORIGINAL CARRABBA'S

Johnny Carrabba is a Houston legend, and one sweetheart of a guy. This soup makes us swoon. It's rich and delicious, and oh-so-satisfying. You might not think of going to Carrabba's just for soup, but maybe you should.

Recipe Notes: This is a great recipe to utilize leftover rind from Parmigiano Reggiano cheese during the last phase to impart even more savory flavor. Johnny's uncle's sausage featured a good amount of fennel, so if the sausage you're using seems light (or missing) fennel seed, add a teaspoon.

YIELD: 12 SERVINGS

Pick through the lentils, and remove any stones or foreign matter.

Rinse the lentils thoroughly, using a fine mesh pasta strainer.

Soak the lentils in cold water, for 40 minutes.

Place the onion, carrots, celery and garlic in food processor, or manually chop to a small dice.

Heat the oil over medium heat, in a large sauté pan.

Add the onion, carrot, celery, garlic and pancetta, and reduce the heat to low.

Stir with a large spoon, until soft, about 10 to 15 minutes. Don't worry about the fond building at the bottom of the pan - it will come off when you add the tomatoes, and even more when you add the chicken broth.

Remove the sausage from the casing, and break it into coarse pieces.

Add the sausage and cook another 5 minutes, or until the sausage is browned.

Add the tomatoes, and cook for 3 minutes more.

Add the lentils and remaining ingredients to a large stockpot, and bring to a boil.

Reduce the heat to low, and simmer uncovered (skimming any foam that rises to the top), for 30 to 35 minutes, or until the lentils are done.

Discard the bay leaf before serving.

1½ cups	dry lentils
1½ cups	yellow onion
1¾ cups	carrot, peeled, trimmed
¼ cup	celery
1 Tbsp	garlic, peeled
¼ cup	olive oil
1½ oz	pancetta, ¼-inch dice
12 oz	sausage links, mild Italian
2 cups	tomatoes, ¼-inch dice
¾ tsp	oregano, dried
1	bay leaf
2¾ Tbsp	parsley leaves
8 cups	chicken stock
1 tsp	red pepper, crushed
1¾ tsp	kosher salt
¾ tsp	black pepper

Wine: A Willamette Valley Pinot Noir, with aromas of cherry and cinnamon
Beer: A malty, sweet IPA, like Simple Malt IPA, from Brasseurs Illimités

HANGOVER
ANDES CAFÉ

Chef David Guerrero is a beloved member of the Houston food community and one incredibly talented chef. This fish soup, from his native Ecuador, is a revelation that features the flavors of cumin, tomatoes and peppers, topped with red onions. It can be served for breakfast, lunch and dinner and is touted as a hangover cure.

Recipe Notes: This soup may be created with any type of seafood. Yuca (or cassava) is a root vegetable and is available at most grocery stores, fresh or frozen.

YIELD: 6 SERVINGS

I Tbsp	vegetable oil
I	tomato, diced
¼	red onion, diced
½ tsp	chili powder
½	red bell pepper, seeded, chopped
I tsp	ground cumin
I tsp	salt
8 cups	water
3	cilantro sprigs
I lb	fresh tuna
½ lb	yuca, fresh or frozen, peeled, sliced
to taste	salt
	red onion, thinly sliced, *for garnish*
	cilantro leaves, *for garnish*
	limes, halved, *for garnish*
	plantain chips, *for garnish*
	popcorn, *for garnish*
	ketchup, *for garnish*
	mustard, *for garnish*
	olive oil, *for garnish*

Heat the oil in a stockpot, over medium heat.

Add the tomatoes, onion, chili powder, bell pepper, cumin and salt.

Add the water, cilantro and tuna.

Increase the heat, and bring to a boil. Cook for 5 minutes.

Strain and remove the tuna, reserving the broth and vegetables. Set the tuna aside.

Add half of the broth and the vegetables to a blender. Purée until smooth.

Add the puréed mixture back into the remaining strained broth.

Bring to a boil over medium-high heat, and add the yuca.

Reduce the temperature, and cook until tender but firm, (30 to 40 minutes for fresh, 15 to 20 minutes for frozen yuca).

Cut the tuna into small- to medium-sized pieces.

Add the yuca chunks and tuna pieces to the broth, taste and add salt, if needed.

To serve:

Ladle the soup into serving bowls.

Garnish with red onion, cilantro, limes, plantain chips, popcorn, ketchup, mustard and olive oil.

Wine: A tropical, medium-bodied Chilean Sauvignon Gris
Beer: A very cold, American Adjunct lager, like Cristal, from Peru

MINESTRONE
CIAO BELLO/TONY'S

Minestrone means "big soup" to Italians — and always includes pasta, beans and vegetables. For an outstanding version, think no farther than Tony Vallone. Mr. Vallone's high standards for every aspect of cuisine and service translate into this incredible, robust soup that works well as a starter or as a main course for a light supper.

YIELD: 8 TO 10 SERVINGS

In a large stockpot over medium-high heat, sauté the onions in 3 tablespoons of the olive oil, for 4 minutes.

Add the carrots and celery, and sauté for 2 minutes more.

Add the garlic, and sauté for 1 minute more.

Add the bouillon cubes, Parmesan rind and prosciutto bone or trimmings to the water.

Add the sautéed mixture of vegetables, and the remaining olive oil.

Increase the temperature to bring to a boil, cover, and then lower the heat.

Let simmer for 1 hour.

Add the drained beans, and let simmer, covered, for 30 minutes.

Add the zucchini, tomatoes and cabbage, and let simmer for 20 minutes.

Add the parsley, oregano or marjoram, sea salt and black pepper, to taste, and simmer for 5 minutes more.

Add more water if needed, but the soup should be thick.

To serve:

Put the hot, al dente pasta in soup bowls, about 1½ cups per bowl.

Pour the soup, and stir in 1 more teaspoon of olive oil per bowl.

Top with grated Parmesan Reggiano, and serve with grilled Italian bread.

1 cup	onions, chopped
6 Tbsp	extra-virgin Italian olive oil
3	carrots, diced
3	celery stalks, sliced
4	garlic cloves, minced
6	chicken bouillon cubes
1	Parmesan rind, (generous piece)
1	prosciutto bone with a little meat on it (optional)
4 qt	water
2 cans	cannellini beans (15-oz), drained
2 cans	red kidney beans (15-oz), drained
2 cans	fava beans (15-oz), drained
3 cups	zucchini, diced
2 cups	tomatoes, peeled and chopped
4 cups	cabbage, shredded (optional)
3 Tbsp	parsley, minced
1 Tbsp	oregano or marjoram, dried
1 Tbsp	sea salt
1½-2 tsp	black pepper, freshly ground
¾ cup	Parmesan Reggiano, grated
1 lb	Tubetti or small pasta, pre-cooked al dente
8-10 tsp	olive oil, *for garnish* Parmesan Reggiano, *for garnish* grilled Italian bread

Wine: A dry, Sangiovese, with aromas of dried herbs and cherries on the palate
Beer: An IPA, like Borgo della Birra "ReAle"

CUCUMBER GAZPACHO
BERNADINE'S

Chef Graham Laborde is one of our favorite chefs and we are madly in love with the food at Bernadine's. Our first taste of this soup left us with arms waving overhead, cheering in our seats.

Recipe Notes: If you don't have lemon vinegar, you may substitute more lemon juice, but the vinegar really makes it sing. You may find lemon vinegar at H-Mart. You may fold in a little bit of sour cream in place of the xanthan gum, to help hold the soup together.

YIELD: 4 TO 6 SERVINGS

SOUP

8	cucumbers
I cup	buttermilk
I¾ tsp	fresh dill
2 Tbsp	parsley leaves
¾ tsp	garlic powder
½ Tbsp	lemon juice
½ Tbsp	lemon vinegar
I Tbsp	kosher salt
¼ tsp	white pepper
I Tbsp	pickled jalapeños
½ tsp	xanthan gum
I Tbsp	water

PICKLED JALAPEÑOS

10	jalapeños
2 tsp	salt
I cup	white vinegar
I cup	water
2 tsp	honey or sugar

cucumber strands, shaved, *for garnish*
pickled jalapeños, *for garnish*
blue crab meat, spoonful, *for garnish*
Persian cucumber, small dice, *for garnish*
queso fresco, sprinkle, *for garnish*

For the soup:

Peel the cucumbers, remove the seeds, and give them a rough chop.

Add to a blender, and purée until smooth.

Strain through a sieve.

Add the cucumber purée, buttermilk, dill, parsley, garlic powder, lemon juice, lemon vinegar, salt, pepper and jalapeño to a blender.

Purée until smooth.

Mix the xanthan gum with 1 tablespoon of water, stirring well, to make a slurry. Add the slurry to the blender and mix well.

Refrigerate the soup, until ready to serve.

For the pickled jalapeños:

Thinly slice the jalapeños.

In a small saucepan over medium-high heat, combine the jalapeños, salt, white vinegar, water and honey (or sugar).

Bring to a boil, and reduce the heat.

Simmer for 15 minutes.

Cool to room temperature, then refrigerate until ready to use.

To serve:

Pour the chilled soup into serving bowls.

Add the cucumber strands, pickled jalapeños, blue crab, cucumber and top with queso fresco.

Wine: A brut sparkling wine, with bright acidity and ripe fruit flavor
Beer: A pilsner malt, like Saint Arnold 5 O'Clock Pils

TORTILLA
GRACE'S

This awesome tortilla soup won us over after many-a-tasting to discover our favorite version. We were smitten with the lush broth and bright, clean flavors within at Grace's, named for Johnny Carrabba's grandmother; a sweet place with a rich Houston history.

YIELD: 6 SERVINGS

1 lb	chicken breasts, skin-on, bone-in
2 tsp	black pepper
1 Tbsp	kosher salt
2⅔ Tbsp	extra-virgin olive oil
1 cup	yellow onion, diced
½ cup	jalapeño, chopped
2 Tbsp	garlic, chopped
2⅓ Tbsp	chicken base
½ tsp	ground cumin
2 cups	whole, peeled tomatoes (15-oz can)
8 cups	cold water
4	corn tortillas
3 cups	olive oil, *for frying*
	olive oil spray, *for oven-frying*
½ tsp	kosher salt
	jalapeño jack cheese, *for garnish*
	avocado chunks, *for garnish*
	cilantro leaves, *for garnish*
	lime wedges, *for garnish*

For the soup:

Generously season the chicken breasts with half of the salt and pepper.

Heat the olive oil in a large skillet, over medium-high heat.

Brown the chicken, for 10 to 20 minutes.

Add the onion, jalapeños and garlic to the pan. Cook for 5 minutes.

Add the chicken base, cumin and tomatoes. Cook for 5 minutes.

Add the water to the stockpot, and bring to a boil.

Add the remaining salt and pepper, and simmer for 45 minutes. Skim any visible fat off the surface of the soup, every 15 minutes.

Remove the chicken from the pot. When cool enough to handle, remove the skin and debone, keeping the chicken meat in large chunks.

Reduce the heat to low, and simmer until reduced. Return the chicken to the soup.

For the tortilla strips:

To fry:

Cut the corn tortillas into 1-inch squares. Heat the oil to 350°F in a deep saucepan, add the tortilla strips, and fry until golden brown. Drain on paper towels. Lightly season with kosher salt.

To oven-fry:

Heat oven to 375°F. Cut the corn tortillas into 1-inch squares, spritz with some olive oil and bake for 7 to 10 minutes, until golden brown. Lightly season with kosher salt.

To serve:

Ladle the soup into bowls.

Top with cheese, tortilla strips and avocado.

Garnish with cilantro and lime wedges.

Wine: A smooth, oaky Tempranillo from Rioja
Beer: A German-style Dunkel, like Negro Modelo

GRASS-FED BEEF PHO
RUGGLES BLACK

Grass-fed pho? What-what? Although not a Vietnamese restaurant, this recipe comes from the authentically-Vietnamese chef Thomas Nguyen. We were so excited to learn about it, and thrilled at how delicious it is. We often turn to Ruggles Black for paleo, gluten-free options.

Recipe Notes: The beef will be easier to slice, if it is a little frozen (about 30 minutes in the freezer).

BROTH

3 lb	beef bones
1 gal	water
	ginger (4-inch), sliced lengthwise, bruised
6	bay leaves
1	yellow onion, chopped
3	carrots (large), chopped
3	celery stalks, chopped
8	thyme sprigs
1 tsp	coriander seeds
3	cinnamon sticks
3	star anise
1 Tbsp	rock sugar
to taste	salt and pepper
to taste	fish sauce

EGGS

4 cups	water
4	eggs
1 lb	rice noodles
1 lb	grass-fed beef tenderloin, thinly sliced
½ cup	micro-basil leaves
½ cup	mint leaves
½ cup	red onion, thinly sliced
½ cup	cilantro leaves
½ cup	jalapeño slices
	scallions, thinly sliced, *for garnish*
	Sriracha, *for garnish*
	chili oil, *for garnish*

YIELD: 4 SERVINGS

For the broth:

Heat the oven to 375˚F.

Put the bones in a large stockpot and cover with water. Bring to a boil, and let it continue to boil for 5 minutes. Turn off the heat when it looks like no more scum is being released. Rinse the bones in a colander.

Place the bones and the ginger on a sheet pan. Roast in the oven for 1 hour, turning once.

Put the bones and ginger in a stockpot, and add the water.

Add the bay leaves, onion, carrot, celery and the thyme sprigs.

Bring to a boil, and reduce to a simmer, for 3 to 4 hours.

Add the coriander, cinnamon sticks and star anise to a skillet set over a medium-low flame. Once the spices are fragrant, remove them from the heat. Lightly crush them, using the flat side of a knife, or mortar and pestle. Encase them in cheesecloth, and add to the broth.

Simmer the broth for another hour.

Strain the broth. Add the sugar, and season to taste with salt, pepper and fish sauce.

Cool down before refrigerating, if not using immediately. If not, keep simmering.

For the eggs:

Bring a medium pot of water to a boil, then reduce to a simmer. Add the eggs, and cook them for 6 minutes.

Remove the eggs, and place them in an ice bath (bowl filled with ice water). Peel the eggs when cool.

To serve:

If using dried noodles, soak them in hot water for 30 minutes

Add the noodles to serving bowls.

Add the beef, and ladle the steaming broth over it. The broth will cook the meat.

Add the basil, mint, onion, cilantro and jalapeño slices.

Add the egg, and garnish with scallions, Sriracha and a little chili oil.

Wine:	A dry Alsatian Riesling
Beer:	A pale lager, like Kingfisher

DUCK ANDOUILLE GUMBO
PROHIBITION SUPPERCLUB & BAR

Although Chef Mike McElroy no longer lives here in Houston, the memory of his grandma's gumbo recipe lives on. We tasted a lot of gumbo before we settled on this one. When it was taken off of the menu for seasonal reasons, we were tagged in a post noting customer rebellion. It's that good.

Recipe Notes: This gumbo is equally delicious made with chicken and sausage. We are big fans of Fatworks brand, pastured pork leaf lard or the pastured pork lard available at Revival Market for the roux.

YIELD: 8 TO 10 SERVINGS

In a heavy bottom pot, bring pork fat to smoking point over high heat.

Slowly whisk in the flour, and stir rapidly until you reach the desired color of dark chocolate (and when you think you're there, keep going a little longer).

Add the onion, celery and poblano, and turn off the heat. Stir until the vegetables are translucent.

(The vegetables will stop the roux from overcooking).

Add the serrano, garlic and country ham, and stir for 1 minute.

Slowly add the hot stock, and bring to a simmer, over medium heat.

Skim the fat and scum off the top, and continue to simmer over low-medium heat, for about an hour.

Add the wet and dry seasoning, and continue to skim and simmer, for another 30 minutes.

Add salt, to taste.

To serve:

Add the cooked meats and the okra to the hot gumbo, and simmer for 5 minutes.

Ladle into serving bowls, and top with cooked rice and green onions.

1¼ lb	pork fat (lard)
1¼ lb	flour
1 qt	onion, medium dice
2 cups	celery, medium dice
2 cups	poblano pepper, medium dice
2	serrano pepper, brunoise (very small cubes)
¼ cup	garlic, chopped
½ cup	country ham, minced
4 qt	pork stock, hot
1 Tbsp	smoked paprika
1 Tbsp	dark chili powder
1 Tbsp	black pepper
1 Tbsp	white pepper
2 Tbsp	salt
1 Tbsp	cayenne
10	bay leaves
1 Tbsp	smoked paprika
½ cup	Crystal hot sauce
½ cup	Worcestershire sauce
to taste	salt
1½ lb	andouille sausage, cooked, cut into half-moons
1½ lb	duck leg meat, roasted, picked
2 cups	charred okra, cut into small rounds
	white rice, cooked
2	green onions, green tops only, chopped, *for garnish*

Wine: An oaked Steen (Chenin Blanc), from South Africa
Beer: A domestic Doppelbock, with hints of caramel, like Consecrator by Bell's Brewery

BEEF BARLEY
THE PALM

This soup is a a classic symbol of nostalgia and tradition at The Palm, where they just celebrated their 38th Anniversary with a major renovation in Houston. Still owned by the original Bozzi and Ganzi families from New York, The Palm continues to serve as a second home for countless patrons and deal makers, alike.

YIELD: 6 SERVINGS

2 Tbsp	extra-virgin olive oil
1 lb	beef sirloin
2	garlic cloves (large), minced
3	celery stalks, small dice
1	white onion (large), small dice
1	carrot (jumbo), peeled, small dice
2 Tbsp	tomato paste
1 cup	red table wine
3 qt	beef stock
1 cup	dry barley
1 tsp	thyme leaves, chopped
2	bay leaves
1	zucchini (large), seeded, small dice
1	yellow squash (large), seeded, small dice
to taste	salt and pepper
	French bread, sliced

Heat the oil in a Dutch oven, over high heat.

Sear the sirloin on both sides; remove the beef, and set aside.

Add the garlic, and sauté with the celery, onions and carrots, 5 to 7 minutes.

Add the tomato paste; cook on low for 7 to 10 minutes, until the paste darkens (this allows the sugars to come up).

Increase the heat to high, and add the red wine to deglaze the pan, using a spatula, and scraping up any browned bits.

When the wine cooks down to very little liquid, add the beef stock, barley, thyme and bay leaves.

Chop the meat, then add to the pot. Simmer on low for 45 minutes.

Then add the zucchini and squash, and remove from heat.

Season to taste, with salt and pepper.

To serve:

Serve with sliced French bread.

Wine: A Malbec, Zinfandel, Syrah or Shiraz
Beer: A Belgian ale, like Duvel, or a stout, like Guinness Draught

CURRIED RED LENTIL
MAIN KITCHEN 806 LOUNGE

Belgian Chef Jelle Vandenbroucke worked at two Michelin-starred restaurants in Europe and the Four Seasons Boston, before becoming executive chef at Main Kitchen 806, within the sexy and historic downtown JW Marriott. This filling soup utilizes fresh ingredients and is very easy to prepare.

Recipe Notes: Chef Jelle's preferred brand of curry paste is Mae Ploy.

YIELD: 6 SERVINGS

For the soup:

In a stockpot over medium-low heat, add the onion and the oil. Sweat until soft, stirring occasionally.

Stir in the red curry paste, and cook for 1 minute.

Add the lemongrass, lime leaves, lentils and the water.

Bring to a boil, turn down to a simmer, and cook for 15 minutes, until lentils are completely soft.

Remove from the heat, and remove the lemongrass and lime leaves.

Add the mixture to a blender, in batches, and process until smooth.

Add the coconut milk and lime juice.

For the mushrooms:

In a saucepot, bring the vegetable stock, vinegar, salt, sugar, mustard seeds and bay leaf to a boil.

When boiling, add the mushrooms and cook for 1 minute.

Take off the heat and let cool. Remove the bay leaf.

Refrigerate and try to store overnight before using. They will keep for about a week.

To serve:

Ladle the soup into bowls.

Add a spoonful of mushrooms, and garnish with snap peas and tarragon leaves.

SOUP

2	yellow onions (medium), diced
1 Tbsp	vegetable oil
3 Tbsp	red curry paste
4	lemongrass stalks, white part only, trimmed, bruised
8	kafir lime leaves
2½ cups	red lentils
5 cups	water
2 cups	coconut milk
2	limes, juiced

MUSHROOMS

1 cup	vegetable stock
1 cup	apple cider vinegar
1 tsp	salt
½ cup	sugar
1 tsp	mustard seeds
1	bay leaf
1 cup	shimeji mushrooms
	sugar snap peas, thinly sliced, *for garnish*
	tarragon leaves, *for garnish*

Wine: A crisp Chardonnay

Beer: A Belgian ale or white, like Fat Tire Amber Ale, from New Belgium Brewing

Good Dog just opened its second location in Montrose, in addition to their original spot in the Heights. Obviously known for their superb hot dogs, their other fare is killer, too! We also love the wild-caught fish and chips plate, and this crazy-good soup.

Recipe Notes: Chef Amalia likes to use 1836 Buffalo Bayou Copper Ale but if that's not available, a medium ale will work. This soup can be made vegetarian simply by not garnishing with bacon.

YIELD: 2 QUARTS

½ cup	unsalted butter
1 cup	carrots, small dice
1 cup	celery, small dice
1 cup	onion, small dice
pinch	salt and pepper
¾ cup+ 1 Tbsp	all-purpose flour
1¼ tsp	mustard powder
¼ tsp	cayenne pepper
1 tsp	Worcestershire sauce
2 cups	beer
1 qt	vegetable stock
2 cups	heavy cream
2 cups	Gruyère cheese, shredded
4 cups	sharp cheddar cheese, shredded
to taste	salt and pepper
	potatoes, boiled, small dice, *for garnish*
	bacon, *for garnish*
	Italian parsley, *for garnish*

In a large enameled cast iron pot, over medium-high heat, add the butter, vegetables, and a pinch of salt and pepper.

Sauté until fragrant, and the onions are translucent, about 5 to 7 minutes.

Combine the flour, mustard powder and cayenne pepper, and add to the sautéed vegetables.

Stir, then add the Worcestershire sauce. Stir and cook, until combined thoroughly.

Add the beer, stirring thoroughly to remove any lumps.

Cook for several minutes, allowing the alcohol to cook out a bit.

Add the vegetable stock, heavy cream, and another pinch of salt. Bring the mixture to a boil.

Slowly whisk in the cheeses, about handful at a time. It is important to do this in small amounts and wait until the soup has returned to a boil, before adding another small amount of cheese.

After all of the cheeses are whisked in, allow the soup to return to a boil once more.

Reduce the heat to medium, and simmer, stirring often, for 10 minutes.

Remove from the heat, and allow to cool.

Add the mixture to a blender and process until smooth (a Vitamix makes it especially velvety!). Season to taste, with salt and pepper, if necessary.

To serve:

Ladle the soup into cups or bowls (soup must be served hot).

Garnish with potatoes, bacon and parsley.

Wine: A medium-dry Alsatian Gewürztraminer
Beer: A medium ale, like 1836 Buffalo Bayou Copper Ale

OYSTER STEW
LIBERTY KITCHEN & OYSTERETTE

Now with four locations in Houston, Liberty Kitchen is known for their great selection of the freshest oysters from everywhere, which makes for a glorious oyster stew. We particularly relish time at the bar of the San Felipe location, enjoying a glass of bubbles to accompany whatever we may find ourselves noshing on. Erin loves to have king crab with her bubbles!

YIELD: 4 SERVINGS

1	sweet potato (large)
1 qt	heavy cream
4 Tbsp	unsalted butter
1⅛ cups	fennel, diced
12	shucked oysters
to taste	salt and pepper
4	fennel fronds, *for garnish* oyster crackers, *for garnish*

Heat oven to 400˚F.

Roast the sweet potato for 45 minutes to 1 hour, until soft.

Remove the skin, and immediately mash the hot potato.

In a medium saucepan, add the cream over medium-high heat, and reduce by half.

Heat the butter in a skillet over medium heat, and sauté the fennel until soft, about 5 to 10 minutes.

Add the oysters, and cook for 20 seconds. Add to the cream mixture.

Season to taste, with salt and pepper.

To serve:

Warm four bowls.

Add a couple of spoonfuls of hot mashed sweet potato to each bowl.

Divide the oysters and cream mixture evenly.

Garnish with fennel fronds. Serve with oyster crackers.

Wine: A Sauvignon Blanc, from coastal regions of the southern hemisphere (Chile, western S. Africa, North Island New Zealand)
Beer: An English stout, like Perle Al Porci from Birra Del Borgo

TOM YUM
SONGKRAN THAI KITCHEN/GRILL

Songkran now boasts two locations in town - the original at Uptown Park and a second in the Land of Sugar. Chef Jett Hurapan has a way with authentic Thai flavors. Jodie traveled to Thailand a couple of years ago (you guessed it, to eat) and she's crazy about this version of the Thai classic.

Recipe Notes: Nam prik pao (roasted red chili paste in soybean oil) and galangal can be purchased at most Asian markets.

YIELD: 4 SERVINGS

½ lb	wild-caught shrimp (large)
6 cups	water
4	lemongrass stalks (4-inch), bruised
½ cup	cilantro stems
1	galangal (2-inch), peeled, chopped
5	kafir lime leaf
1 tsp	nam prik pao (roasted red chili paste)
8	straw mushrooms
8	cherry tomatoes
2 tsp	fish sauce
2 Tbsp	lime juice
4	Thai chiles, *for garnish* green onions, *for garnish* cilantro leaves, *for garnish*

Peel and devein the shrimp and set aside, reserving the shells for the broth.

Fill a stockpot with water.

Add the shrimp shells, lemongrass, cilantro, galangal, lime leaves and chili paste.

Bring to a boil, then lower the heat, and let simmer for 30 minutes.

Strain the broth. Add the raw shrimp, mushrooms, tomatoes, fish sauce and lime juice.

Cook for 5 to 10 minutes, on medium heat.

To serve:

Ladle the soup into serving bowls.

Garnish with Thai chiles, green onions and cilantro.

Wine: An Oregon Riesling, with racy acidity and nectarine and apricot flavors
Beer: A pale lager, like Tsingtao

VEGAN CHILI
LOCAL FOODS

Let us be completely honest here: We were unfamiliar with textured vegetable protein (aka TVP) until we saw this recipe. Had to google it, in fact. Don't be afraid of it. You would not think it was vegan unless you'd seen the recipe. Chef Dylan Murray does a fine job with beautiful ingredients and fresh flavors, at Local Foods.

Recipe Notes: You may substitute a dried ancho for the pasilla chile. Use the same recipe, with a small amount of water, for great vegan taco meat or for an 8-layer dip! You may use canned or dried navy beans. If using dried, soaked beans, you will need to cook the chili for an extra hour. There are instructions for pickling onions and toasting pumpkin seeds on page 131.

YIELD: 10 SERVINGS

Purée the pasilla peppers with ¼ cup water. Set aside.

Add the olive oil to a large stockpot, over medium-low heat.

Add the onion, tomatoes, poblanos, peppers, garlic, oregano and the bay leaf, and sweat them until they become translucent, about 10 to 15 minutes.

Add the TVP, yeast, beans, ketchup, cumin, cayenne, paprika, chili powder, and the remaining water.

Bring to a boil, and simmer for about an hour.

Remove the bay leaf.

To serve:

Ladle the chili into serving bowls.

Top with pickled onions, cilantro leaves and pumpkin seeds.

¾	pasilla pepper, dried, seeded, membranes removed
1¾ Tbsp	extra-virgin olive oil
1¾ cups	white onion, julienned
3¼ cups	tomatoes, large dice
⅔ cup	poblanos, seeded, large dice
⅔ cup	red bell pepper, seeded, large dice
1¾ Tbsp	garlic, minced
1¾ Tbsp	oregano, chopped
1	bay leaf
1¾ cup	textured vegetable protein (TVP)
⅓ cup	nutritional yeast
¼ cup	navy beans (canned)
¼ cup	ketchup
1 tsp	ground cumin
½ tsp	cayenne pepper
¼ Tbsp	paprika
⅓ tsp	chili powder
6¼ cups	water
to taste	salt
	pickled onions, *for garnish*
	cilantro leaves, *for garnish*
	pumpkin seeds, toasted, *for garnish*

Wine: A Russian River Pinot Noir with aromas of dark cherry and dried flowers
Beer: A Belgian-style witbier, like Bière du vexin Blanche

MUSHROOM-KOMBU
OXHEART

James Beard Award winner Chef Justin Yu is a culinary genius. His warehouse district gem, Oxheart, has gathered a slew of awards and loyal followers with dishes like this sublime soup, that screams with umami flavors.

Recipe Notes: Kombu is dry seaweed. Miso is fermented soybean paste that is available in the refrigerated section of most grocery stores.

Justin steams 20 pounds of mushrooms overnight in the oven, then strains them through a cheesecloth to obtain the mushroom broth. We found that using a good organic mushroom broth (Pacific brand from Whole Foods or online) worked great for our quicker version of this recipe, but you could certainly make the mushroom broth from scratch.

YIELD: 6 SERVINGS

KOMBU BROTH

⅛ oz	kombu (3- by 4-inch)
1 cup	water
6 cups	mushroom broth
3 Tbsp	miso, shiro or awase
2 Tbsp	soy sauce
2 Tbsp	mirin
4 oz	white button mushrooms, sliced, *for garnish*
1	green onion, sliced, *for garnish*
	kombu strips, *for garnish*

To make the kombu broth:

Add the kombu and the water to a small pot.

Bring up to a simmer from cold, over medium heat.

(The white substance you'll see coming up is just salt from the seaweed. Don't worry!).

Remove from the heat. Cover, and let steep for 1 hour.

Remove the kombu, and let cool.

When cool, thinly slice the kombu, for garnish.

Mix the mushroom and kombu broths in a medium pot, and bring to a boil, over medium-high heat.

Whisk in the miso, and remove from the heat.

Season with soy sauce and mirin.

Garnish with raw or cooked mushrooms, green onions and kombu strips.

Wine: A ripe, fruity, high acid, Gamay, from Fleurie, Beaujolais
Beer: A funky, spicy Trappist ale, like Orval, from Belgium

CHICKEN MATZO BALL
KENNY & ZIGGY'S

Jewish penicillin is what they call it - and for good reason. If anybody even starts feeling sick, we head straight for this soup, stat (and it's not bad when you're feeling great, either). Ziggy Gruber, star of the documentary "Deli Man," gave us his family's recipe, which is about as authentic as it gets. People will love you for this one.

Recipe Notes: If you don't have schmaltz, don't schvitz!! It's just rendered chicken fat. You can substitute vegetable oil for the schmaltz. Other options for the matzo balls: cooked noodles, rice or kasha. Be sure to use onions with a firm, golden-brown peel.

YIELD: ½ GALLON

For the soup:

Place all of the ingredients in a large stockpot and cover with water, on the stove, on medium-high.

Let the soup simmer for 1 hour and 15 minutes.

Remove the chicken. When the chicken cools, cut it into bite-sized pieces. (You can add it to the soup, just before serving, or save it for chicken salad).

Strain the soup, and discard everything solid except for the carrots and celery.

Add salt and pepper, to taste. Slice the carrots and celery. Toss into the soup. Add the chicken, if desired.

For the matzo balls:

Crack the eggs into a large bowl, and beat with a fork to mix thoroughly. Beat in the schmaltz, and add a ¼ teaspoon of the salt and the pepper.

Stir in the matzo meal, and mix vigorously with a wooden spoon, until completely blended and very stiff. Let stand for 30 minutes. It may be refrigerated, covered with plastic wrap, until ready to use (up to 8 hours).

Fill a large wide pot ¾ full with water. Add the remaining tablespoon of salt, and bring to a boil over high heat. Wet your hands with cold water (so the batter doesn't stick to them), then holding and rolling the mixture between your palms, shape it into perfect balls, about 1¼-inches in diameter. They will double in size when cooked.

Gently place the matzo balls in the boiling water. When all have been added, decrease the heat so the water simmers briskly, but isn't at a rolling boil, when the pot is covered.

Cover and cook for 25 minutes, preferably without removing the pot lid. Remove the cooked matzo balls with a slotted spoon.

Serve in the hot chicken soup.

SOUP

1	whole chicken
3	celery stalks, chopped
1	onion (large), unpeeled
2	carrots (large), peeled
1	dill bunch, cleaned, tied with a string
1	parsley bunch, cleaned, tied with a string
to taste	kosher salt
¼ tsp	pepper

MATZO BALLS

4	eggs (large)
⅓ cup	schmaltz (rendered chicken fat)
¼ tsp+ 1 Tbsp	salt
¼ tsp	white or black pepper, freshly ground (preferably white)
1⅓ cups	matzo meal

Wine: A structured Rosé, full of citrus and minerality, from Bandol
Beer: A lemon-zesty saison, farmhouse-style, like Brooklyn Brewery Iconic Sorachi Ace

BLACK BEAN
HUNGRY'S CAFÉ

Hungry's has been around since 1975. Now with two locations, including the new ginormous Rice location with its big lounge. Their globally-inspired, made-from-scratch menu includes this hearty vegetarian soup, which is an award-winning family recipe.

YIELD: 6 TO 8 SERVINGS

SOUP

1 lb	black beans, dried
¾ cup	yellow onions, chopped
1 cup	green bell pepper, seeded, chopped
2½ tsp	garlic, chopped
½	jalapeño pepper, seeded, chopped (optional)
5 tsp	olive oil
1 tsp	cumin powder
1	bay leaf
1 Tbsp	fresh oregano
to taste	salt and pepper

PICO DE GALLO

¼ cup	white onion, chopped
1 Tbsp	cilantro, chopped
1 cup	tomatoes, chopped
½ Tbsp	jalapeño, chopped, with seeds
⅛ tsp	garlic powder
½ Tbsp	lime juice
to taste	salt and pepper

For the soup:

Soak the beans in enough water to cover, overnight.

Strain and rinse the beans, removing any dirt or rocks.

In a large stockpot, cover the beans with about 4 inches of water, and bring to a boil.

Reduce the temperature to medium-low and simmer, partially covered, for about 1½ hours, or until tender.

In a skillet over medium heat, sauté the onion, bell pepper, garlic and jalapeño with the olive oil, and add the cumin, bay leaf and oregano, for 5 to 10 minutes.

Add the sautéed mixture to the beans, and simmer on low heat, for 45 minutes. Remove the bay leaf.

Season to taste, with salt and pepper.

For the pico de gallo:

Combine all the ingredients in a bowl. Mix well.

To serve:

Ladle the soup into bowls.

Top with a spoonful of pico de gallo.

Wine: A medium-bodied, rustic red, like Tempranillo or Sangiovese
Beer: A Hefeweizen, like Live Oak Hefeweizen

GREEN BEAN
BORGO FOOD STATION

Talented chef Monica Fallone shops for her ingredients at farmer's markets and through local sustainable purveyors, which is exactly how we want to eat. No wonder everything here is so fresh and delicious, and this soup is no exception. Don't miss Borgo's housemade pastas and antipasti, either. This is what takeout should be.

Recipe Notes: Be sure to use fresh green beans and thyme. You may add more potato to thicken the soup, if necessary. I used organic vegetable stock from Trader Joe's and the result was fantastic, although there's a great vegetable stock recipe on page 136. Chicken stock will also work in this recipe - just adjust the seasoning accordingly.

YIELD: 6 SERVINGS

Preheat the oven to 350°F.

Drizzle the olive oil over a sheet pan.

Add the garlic, celery, onion, thyme and potatoes, and toss to coat.

Cook for 10 to 15 minutes, stirring occasionally, until soft and golden-colored.

In a large pot, bring the stock to a boil, add the oven-roasted vegetables and the green beans.

Cook for 30 minutes, over medium to low heat, or until the beans are soft.

Pull out half of the potatoes, and set aside. Put the rest of the vegetables in the blender.

Add the stock, and blend until smooth. Add more potatoes, if necessary, to thicken the soup.

Add salt and pepper, to taste, to balance the flavor.

To serve:

Garnish with a drizzle of olive oil, thyme sprigs and crunchy green beans.

2 Tbsp	extra-virgin olive oil
1	garlic clove, peeled
1	celery stalk, trimmed
1	onion (medium), peeled, chopped
½ tsp	thyme leaves
2	red potatoes, peeled, cut in half
6 cups	vegetable stock
1 lb	green beans
to taste	sea salt and black pepper, freshly ground
drizzle	olive oil, *for garnish*
	thyme sprigs, *for garnish*
	crunchy green beans, *for garnish*

Wine: A Müller-Thurgau, from Alto Adige, with a nose of muscat sweetness, lemon zest and a dry finish

Beer: An IPA, like Ballast Point Even Keel Session IPA, with balanced malt and hops, and citrus and herbal notes

CORN CHOWDER
RUGGLES GREEN

Ruggles Green has set itself apart and led the way in the organic movement, here in Houston. It's plumb exciting that they have locations throughout the city now.

Recipe Notes: We like reserving a little of the corn mixture to use as a garnish - texture makes the world go 'round! It's important to note that they only use organic corn at Ruggles Green, which is often difficult to find fresh. If you can't find fresh organic corn, look for organic canned or frozen corn.

YIELD: 8 SERVINGS

1⅔ Tbsp	olive oil
1	red bell pepper, seeded, chopped
2	yellow bell pepper, seeded, chopped
½ cup	celery, diced
¼	jalapeño with seeds, chopped
⅔ cup	yellow onion (medium), chopped
2 Tbsp	cilantro leaves, chopped
1¼ tsp	salt
1 tsp	black pepper
6 cups	vegetable stock
2 Tbsp	chicken base
1 lb	corn, fresh or canned
2⅓ cups	heavy cream
	truffle oil, *for garnish*

Heat the olive oil in a stockpot, over medium heat.

Add the red and yellow bell pepper, celery, jalapeño, onion and cilantro.

Sauté until translucent, about 10 to 15 minutes.

Add the salt, pepper, vegetable stock, chicken base and corn.

Bring to a boil, then reduce to simmer for 30 to 45 minutes, until thick.

Add the heavy cream, and reduce for about 20 minutes more.

Add the mixture to a blender, and purée until smooth.

To serve:

Ladle the soup into serving bowls.

Garnish with a few drops of truffle oil, if desired.

Wine: A New Zealand-style Sauvignon Blanc, or a dry German or French Riesling with minerality
Beer: A German Dortmunder-style lager, like Oak Highlands Brewery Golden Mustache

RAMEN
IZAKAYA

We're crazy about Izakaya's whole menu and Chef Philippe's ramen is some of the best in the city.

Recipe Notes: Most ingredients may be found at Super H-Mart or online. Save time by making the stock in advance, and though Chef Philippe makes his own roasted pork belly, we opted for a short-cut version using grilled pork tenderloin (which may also be made ahead of time) with great results. Remember, all the other ingredients will be added to the noodles and stock, so use reasonably large bowls for serving.

YIELD: 6 SERVINGS

For the tonakatsu stock:

Place the pig feet, onion, carrots, and celery in a large stockpot, and add the water. Bring to a boil, and then simmer, for 4 to 5 hours. Strain and reserve.

For the pork tenderloin:

Heat the oven to 400°F. Rub the tenderloin with the Togarashi seasoning and salt. Melt the lard in a hot cast iron skillet, and sear the tenderloin on both sides. Place the tenderloin in the oven, and roast for approximately 20 minutes, flipping the tenderloin halfway through, until you reach an internal temp of 140 to 145°F for medium-rare. Keep in mind the tenderloin will continue to cook as it rests, when removed from the oven. Let the tenderloin rest for about 10 to 15 minutes, before thinly slicing.

For the eggs:

Bring a medium pot of water to a boil, then reduce to a simmer. Add the eggs, and cook them for 6 minutes. Remove the eggs, and place them in an ice bath (bowl filled with ice and water). Peel the eggs when cool.

To serve:

Bring the stock to a boil. In a separate pot, boil the water and cook the noodles for exactly 2 minutes. Drain and put the noodles in the boiling stock for another minute. Pull the noodles and place them in large bowls.

To the boiling stock, add the garlic/ginger mix, the butter and the pork base until the butter melts. Ladle the stock over the noodles. Slice the soft-boiled egg in half, and place alongside the fish cake, pickles, wakame, green onions and the pork slices, all in separate little mounds, around the egg.

Sprinkle a pinch of sesame seeds on each serving, drizzle with a little sesame oil, and sprinkle with Togarashi seasoning.

Wine: A New Zealand-style Sauvignon Blanc
Beer: A Belgian white ale, like Hitachino Nest

STOCK

2	pig feet, raw
1	yellow onion (jumbo), chopped
2	carrots (jumbo), chopped
4	celery stalks, chopped
1 gal	water

PORK TENDERLOIN

2 lb	pork tenderloin
4 Tbsp	Togarashi (Japanese Five Spice)
2 tsp	salt
2 Tbsp	pork lard or bacon grease

EGGS

6 cups	water
6	eggs
6	fresh ramen noodle packs
2 Tbsp	garlic and ginger root mix, minced
6 Tbsp	unsalted butter
6 Tbsp	somi paitan (ramen-concentrated pork base)
12 oz	wakame (seaweed), rehydrated
24	naruto maki (fish cake) slices
1½ cups	green onions, sliced
12 oz	fukujinzuke (Japanese pickled daikon and cabbage)
24	roasted pork tenderloin slices
⅓ tsp	sesame seeds
2 Tbsp	sesame oil
sprinkle	Togarashi spice, *for garnish*

TOM KA GAI
FOREIGN CORRESPONDENTS

Lauded as one of Bon Appetit's 50 Best New Restaurants in the nation, Foreign Correspondents is Houston's only farm-to-table Northern and Northeastern Thai restaurant. Exciting Thai dishes are paired with German Rieslings and an innovative Thai-inspired cocktail list for an thrilling addition to Houston's dining scene.

Recipe Notes: Galangal may be purchased at most Asian markets.

YIELD: 4 SERVINGS

1⅛ lb	chicken breast, skinless, boneless
1½ cups	coconut milk
1 cup	chicken broth
⅔ cup	galangal, sliced (3½-oz)
⅓ cup	lemongrass, sliced, white part only
5-10	kafir lime leaves
2 cups	oyster mushrooms
5-10	Thai chiles
3 Tbsp	fish sauce
3 Tbsp	lime juice
to taste	salt
	cilantro, *for garnish*
	green onions, chopped, *for garnish*

Thinly slice the chicken breast into thick ⅛-inch slices, and set aside.

Combine the coconut milk and chicken broth in a pot, then add the galangal, lemongrass and lime leaves.

Bring to a boil, let cook for about 2 to 3 minutes, then add the chicken.

Simmer about 5 minutes.

Add the mushrooms, chiles, fish sauce and lime juice.

Cook until the mushrooms and chicken are done, about 5 to 10 minutes.

Season to taste, with salt.

To serve:

Ladle the soup into serving bowls.

Garnish with cilantro and green onions.

Wine: A bone-dry German Riesling, with aromas of peach, lime and white flowers
Beer: A crisp Kölsch-style or pilsner, like Saint Arnold Fancy Lawnmower or Scrimshaw

CALDO XOCHITL
THE ORIGINAL NINFA'S ON NAVIGATION

This festive soup is also known as Mexican hot flower soup. It's a traditional holiday first course as well as a perfect light lunch. Chef Alex Padilla's mother, Maria, worked for Mama Ninfa Laurenzo as a line cook at Ninfa's in the 1980s - the tradition continues!

Recipe Notes: You may use whatever cuts of chicken you prefer.

YIELD: 6 SERVINGS

Add the water, celery, tomato, onion, bell pepper and chicken to a large stockpot.

Add the bay leaf, salt, cumin, garlic powder and black pepper.

Bring to a boil, then cook for 1 hour, at a slow simmer.

Remove the chicken, and let cool.

Strain out all the vegetables, and keep the stock warm.

When the chicken is cool, debone the meat and tear into large pieces.

Add the chicken back to the pot.

To serve:

Ladle the soup into bowls.

Top with cilantro leaves and garnish with avocado slices, pico de gallo, tortilla strips, and lemon or lime wedges.

2 qt	water
1	celery stalk, chopped
1 cup	tomato (medium), chopped
½ cup	yellow onion, chopped
½	red bell pepper, seeded, chopped
½	green bell pepper, seeded, chopped
2 lb	chicken, bone-in, skinless
1	bay leaf
1 Tbsp	salt
½ Tbsp	ground cumin
½ Tbsp	garlic powder
½ Tbsp	black pepper, freshly ground
¼ cup	cilantro leaves, *for garnish*
	avocado slices, *for garnish*
	pico de gallo, *for garnish*
	tortilla strips, *for garnish*
	lemon or lime wedges, *for garnish*

Wine: A medium-bodied Spanish Rosé, with fruity, vegetal aromas and lively acidity

Beer: A Mexican lager, like Dos Equis - or a Michelada, made with Dos Equis!

ARTICHOKE BISQUE
ROOST

BISQUE

5	globe artichokes (1 lb each) -OR-
1 jar	artichoke hearts (12-oz)
4 Tbsp	extra-virgin olive oil
¾ lb	Yukon gold potatoes, peeled, ½-inch dice
4	shallots (large), peeled, halved
3	garlic cloves (large), peeled, halved
to taste	salt
1 cup	dry white wine
4 cups	chicken stock or broth
4 oz	Parmesan rind
12	thyme sprigs, tied
1 Tbsp	black peppercorns, tied in cheesecloth
½ cup	heavy cream

GRILLED LEMON OIL

1	lemon, cut in half lengthwise
2 cups	extra-virgin olive oil
½ tsp	salt
	artichoke hearts, grilled, sliced, *for garnish*
½ cup	Parmesan shavings, *for garnish*

We like to say, "We knew him when!" From his days as Randy Evans' sous at Haven, chef Kevin Naderi has racked up many accolades and has come up the winner in many competitions - most recently on the Food Network show, "Beating Bobby Flay" where he took the Iron Chef down with his take on cabbage rolls!

Recipe Notes: You may substitute jarred artichoke hearts for the fresh ones. Be sure to make the lemon oil ahead of time - it needs to steep overnight.

YIELD: 4 TO 6 SERVINGS

For the bisque:

If using fresh artichokes: Working with 1 artichoke at a time, snap off the outer leaves. Using a sharp knife, trim the stem and base of the artichoke, and cut off the top two-thirds of the leaves. With a spoon or melon baller, scrape out the furry choke.

If using jarred artichokes: Drain the artichokes and place on a towel to absorb some of their liquid.

Rub the artichoke hearts all over with a tablespoon or two of olive oil. Grill the hearts over an open flame until tender, about 5 minutes. Reserve a couple of the hearts to slice and use as garnish.

Add 2 tablespoons of olive oil to a saucepan over medium heat, and add the potatoes, shallots and garlic; season with salt.

Cook over moderate heat, stirring occasionally, until the vegetables are lightly browned, and barely tender, about 20 minutes.

Add the wine, and cook until nearly evaporated, about 7 minutes. Add the chicken stock, Parmesan rind, thyme bundle and black peppercorns.

Bring to a boil. Cover partially, and cook over moderately low heat, until the vegetables are tender, about 30 minutes. Discard the thyme bundle, peppercorns and Parmesan rind.

Working in batches, purée the soup until smooth. Return it to the saucepan. Add the heavy cream, and season with salt. Keep the soup warm.

For the grilled lemon oil:

Grill the lemon, rind and all, over an open flame until charred.

Place in a small saucepot with the oil and salt, bring to a very light boil and then turn down to low. Allow to cook for 5 minutes. Take off of the heat and allow to steep overnight. Strain the oil and reserve.

To serve:

Ladle the soup into bowls. Mound some Parmesan shavings in the center, and top with grilled artichoke slices.

Wine: A lush and fruity white, like Viognier or Grüner Veltliner
Beer: A dry cider, like Argus Cidery Ciderkin

CHAMPAGNE PUFF PASTRY
RIVER OAKS COUNTRY CLUB

In the 1920s, River Oaks became Houston's first master-planned community, with the country club at its heart. Since then, many a fine meal has been enjoyed within these membership-only walls. This celebratory soup is featured as an elegant starter. It's a simple way to impress, for a first course!

Recipe Notes: Be sure to use wine and champagne you'd like to drink because, well, why wouldn't you?

YIELD: 4 SERVINGS

1 tsp	olive oil
2 Tbsp	onion
½ tsp	garlic, minced
¼	bay leaf
2 Tbsp	white wine, preferably Chablis
½ cup	heavy cream
2 cups	chicken stock
4 oz	Camembert cheese, rind removed, chopped, (room temp)
2 Tbsp	Parmesan cheese, grated
½ tsp	corn starch (mixed with 1 Tbsp cold water, if needed)
2 Tbsp	Champagne
1	puff pastry sheet, thawed
1	egg
2 tsp	heavy cream
	chives, minced, *for garnish*

Add the oil to a large stock pot, over medium-low heat.

Add the onions and garlic, and sweat them for about 5 minutes, until translucent.

Add the bay leaf and wine, and increase the temperature to medium.

Cook until most of the wine has evaporated.

Add the stock and bring to a simmer, for 5 minutes.

Add the cream, stir to combine, and cook for about 10 minutes, until it starts to thicken a up a bit.

Discard the bay leaf.

Add the Camembert and the Parmesan, and stir to melt.

Purée with an immersion blender (or in a blender), until smooth.

Return the soup to the pot. Cook the soup down, over medium heat, to thicken, or you may thicken with the corn starch slurry, if necessary.

Add the champagne last (as to not cook out the flavor) and give it a stir.

Chill the soup down, to room temperature.

Heat the oven to 375°F.

Using your soup cup as the guide, trace around the cup on your puff dough to get the right size.

Fill the soup cups ½ way full, so they don't bubble over in the oven. Crack the egg into a small bowl, and whisk until well blended. Whisk in the heavy cream. Set aside.

Using your palm, flatten out the dough, and place it on top of the soup cup. Using your fingers, press the dough ¼-inch down rim of the soup cup, and crimp to make the dough taught like a drum. Brush the puff pastry with the egg wash.

Place in the oven for 15 minutes.

To serve:

Garnish with minced chives.

Wine: A blanc de blancs Champagne
Beer: A light amber, French Country ale, like Domaine Dupage

SMOKED TOMATO
STATE OF GRACE

State of Grace is one of the most aesthetically and culinarily pleasing restaurants in the whole city - Houston was super happy to welcome chef Ford Fry home! For a fresh take on tomato soup, chef Bobby Matos gave it a smoky edge and added pimento croquettes! Let's just say you want these in your life!

Recipe Notes: Erin also tested this recipe with gluten-free Panko bread crumbs and coconut flour for the croquettes with great success! You may use any kind of wood chips to smoke the tomatoes. There is a recipe for pickled onions on page 131.

YIELD: 4 SERVINGS

For the soup:

Soak the wood chips in water for 30 minutes. Add the chips to an aluminum pan or foil packet. Place on a grill over medium-high heat, until they start to smoke.

Add the tomatoes to another grill pan, and smoke for 30 to 45 minutes, until they develop a bit of color and a heavy smoke aroma.

Heat the olive oil in a medium stockpot over medium-low heat, and cook the garlic and shallots until they start to brown.

Add the smoked and canned tomatoes, and simmer for 20 to 30 minutes, until the tomatoes break down.

Purée the soup (in a blender or using an immersion blender) until smooth, and strain through a sieve into another container.

Continue to purée the soup, while slowly adding the cubed butter, until completely incorporated.

Finish with salt and pepper, to taste.

For the croquettes:

Mix the first 5 ingredients together in a bowl, and fold in the cheeses. Scoop out tablespoon-sized pieces, form into balls, and lay out on a cookie sheet. Place in the freezer for at least 1 hour.

While the pimento balls are in the freezer, set up a 3-part breading station. In the first bowl add the flour. In the second bowl, make an eggwash by mixing together the egg and milk. In the third bowl, add the Panko.

Dredge the frozen balls in the flour. Shake off any excess flour and transfer to the eggwash. Then, transfer to the Panko and press the bread crumbs to completely coat the balls.

In a heavy pot, bring the oil to 350°F. Fry the croquettes in batches. They are done when they begin to float.

To serve:

Place 2 croquettes in a soup bowl, and pour the soup around.

Garnish with pickled onions, scallions, and basil leaves.

Wine: A Sangiovese, with herbal and tomato notes
Beer: A German Kölsch, like Reissdorf Kölsch, or Sunner

SOUP

3 cups	oak wood chips, soaked
2½ lb	red heirloom tomatoes, quartered
¼ cup	olive oil
½ cup	garlic cloves, peeled
1 cup	shallots, peeled, rough chopped
1 can	tomatoes, peeled (15-oz)
¼ lb	unsalted butter, cold, cubed
to taste	salt and pepper

PIMENTO CROQUETTES

1 Tbsp	mayonnaise
1 Tbsp	cream cheese, softened
2 Tbsp	jarred pimento peppers, diced
¾ tsp	Worcestershire sauce
1½ tsp	dill, chopped
2 oz	sharp cheddar cheese, grated
2 oz	extra sharp cheddar cheese, grated
1	egg, beaten
¼ cup	whole milk
½ cup	all-purpose flour
½ cup	Panko bread crumbs
4 cups	oil, *for frying*
	pickled red onions, *for garnish*
	scallions, finely julienned, *for garnish*
	basil leaves, torn, *for garnish*

ITALIAN WEDDING SOUP
ARTHUR AVE

At this fantastic new restaurant in the Heights , beautifully designed by Erin, Chef William Wright translates his Italian culinary training and inspiration into dishes we were instantly obsessed with. The Italian words "minestra maritata" means "married soup", not literal marriage but rather referring to the edible delights that go so well together. Over the years the meaning was construed to be associated with marriage and renamed "wedding soup".

Recipe Notes: Yes, canned cherry tomatoes do exist! Truth be told, they hold up much better in this soup, (but you can use fresh ones, in a pinch). Instructions for roasted garlic paste are on page 54.

YIELD: 6 SERVINGS

ITALIAN MEATBALLS

⅓ cup	milk
2⅓ oz	bread
1 lb	ground beef
1⅔ Tbsp	olive oil
1½ tsp	salt
¾ Tbsp	parsley, chopped
1½ tsp	roasted garlic paste
⅓	yellow onion, grated
¾ Tbsp	oregano, fresh
1 Tbsp	egg, beaten

SOUP

6 cups	vegetable stock
1 cup	garbanzo beans or chickpeas, canned
½ cup	fennel, thinly sliced
1 cup	cherry tomatoes, canned
1 tsp	wild, dried Sicilian or Greek oregano
½ cup	elbow pasta
2 tsp	salt
½ tsp	black pepper, freshly cracked
¼ cup	celery hearts, sliced
1¼ cups	escarole, chopped
½ cup	extra-virgin olive oil
	Parmesan shavings, *for garnish*
	Italian flat leaf parsley, *for garnish*
	celery leaves, *for garnish*

For the Italian meatballs:

Heat the oven to 350°F.

Make a panade, by combining the milk and bread together in the mixing bowl of a stand mixer (or using a hand mixer).

Rest for 10 minutes, to soften. Slowly mix over low speed, until combined.

Add half of the beef to the bowl. Mix on low to medium speed, until completely combined with the panade. The mixture should look very smooth and lighten in color when well emulsified.

Add the olive oil, salt, parsley, garlic paste, onion, oregano and egg, to the mixer and mix over low speed, until just combined.

Fold in the remaining beef by hand. Roll into ½-ounce meatballs, and place on a sheet pan lined with parchment paper.

Bake in the oven for 3 minutes on one side. Flip and bake another 4 minutes. Remove from the oven and set aside.

For the soup:

In a medium-sized stockpot, bring the stock to a simmer, over medium-high heat.

Add the chickpeas, fennel, tomatoes, oregano, pasta, salt and pepper. Cook over medium heat for 5 minutes.

Add the celery hearts, escarole, and the meatballs. Simmer for another 10 minutes

Finish with olive oil and season to taste, with salt and pepper.

To serve:

Garnish with Parmesan shavings, parsley and celery leaves.

Wine:	A soft, cherry-flavored Dolcetto
Beer:	A crisp, clean and refreshing lager, like Peroni Lager

OCTOPUS-CHORIZO-POTATO
CHEF ALVIN SCHULTZ

MasterChef competitor, Alvin Schultz, is a freak-genius in the kitchen, according to Gordon Ramsey. Don't freak out about cooking octopus! This recipe couldn't be simpler - no massaging the octopus, pounding it, soaking it with copper, or cooking it with a wine cork.

Recipe Notes: Octopus quality can vary greatly. You'll want to start with a high quality Mediterranean, or Japanese octopus. In Houston, the best raw octopus comes from Blue Horizon Seafood near Rice Village. Ask Frixtos, the owner, to tell you octopus stories from Greece and clear your schedule for the rest of the day. It's worth the time! Octopus are almost 99.9% edible, which means they'll come free of any organ meats. The only inedible part is the "beak", which is a small hard ball on the underside of the body where the tentacles meet (about the size of a marble). The spice and richness of the chorizo, along with the brininess of the octopus, are challenging to pair with. Alvin's favorite pairing is La Nina Del Mezcal's Tobala varietal from 2014. Its got an amazing palate of epazote and green apple which play off both the parsley and chorizo nicely.

YIELD: 8 SERVINGS

20 oz	Mexican-style chorizo
1	Mediterranean Octopus (4- to 5lb), thawed
1 qt	water
1 qt	red new potatoes (small)
	parsley leaves, *for garnish*
8 Tbsp	sherry vinegar

Remove the chorizo from the casing and put into a cold, large pot. Cook over medium heat to render all of the fat, about 20 minutes. Sausage should crumble. Remove ½ of the sausage and reserve.

Place the octopus in the pot with the remaining chorizo and rendered fat.

Cover and cook over medium heat for about 40 minutes or until a knife easily pierces the thick part of the octopus tentacle. You may have to cook it for up to an hour.

Once the octopus is tender, remove it from the pot and try to brush off any chorizo that's sticking to the octopus. Cut off the octopus head and place the head back in the pot. Cut off and reserve the tentacles. Remove and discard the beak.

Add 1 quart of water and half of the potatoes to the pot with the octopus liquid, chorizo, and fat. Increase the heat to high, and cover. Cook until the potatoes are fork tender, about 20 to 25 minutes.

Transfer the contents of the pot into a high speed blender,and purée until smooth. Pass through a sieve, and keep the soup warm.

Add the remaining potatoes to a glass container. Cover with water, and season with salt. Microwave for 3 to 5 minutes, depending on their size.

Warm the reserved chorizo over medium heat, and add the parboiled potatoes, to cook through.

To serve:

Sear the octopus tentacles in a hot pan or grill. Slice the tentacles. Place in serving bowls with potato, chorizo and parsley. Drizzle with the sherry vinegar.

Pour in the soup. For dramatic effect, pour the soup tableside.

Wine: A heavyweight Roussanne, from northern Rhone that exudes honeysuckle and beeswax
Beer: A malty, complex amber ale, like North Peak Siren

ASPARAGUS CHICKPEA
GIACOMO'S CIBO E VINO

While trendy restaurants come and go, chef-owner Lynette Hawkins' sweet trattoria is consistently appealing for everything from pasta, to beautifully-seasoned roasted meats, and a casual, small-plates mentality.

Recipe Notes: Soak the chickpeas overnight in plenty of water with a pinch of kosher salt and a pinch of baking soda. Make sure to fully caramelize the vegetables - this adds a ton of flavor.

YIELD: 12 CUPS

3	asparagus bunches
14 cups	water
3 cups	yellow onion, finely diced
1½ cups	fennel bulb, finely diced
1 Tbsp	garlic, minced
¼ cup	olive oil
1 Tbsp	kosher salt
¼ tsp	black pepper
1 cup	dried chickpeas, soaked overnight
1	bay leaf
1 Tbsp	fresh tarragon (heaping), chopped
2 Tbsp	fresh Italian parsley, chopped
1 Tbsp	olive oil
pinch	kosher salt
1 Tbsp	white wine

Snap the tough fibrous bottoms off each asparagus spear, and reserve for the broth.

Slice off the asparagus tips, and set them aside for garnish. Finely dice the remaining tender asparagus (you should end up with about 4 cups).

Add the tough asparagus bottoms and water in a stockpot. Bring to a boil, and simmer for about 30 minutes, until the water is fragrant with asparagus.

In a large stockpot, sauté the onion, fennel and garlic in the olive oil with salt and pepper, until completely tender and caramelized, about 30 minutes, stirring constantly.

Drain and rinse the chickpeas. Add the chickpeas and the bay leaf to the pot, and stir to coat the chickpeas with the caramelized vegetables.

Strain the asparagus broth directly into the pot. Cover, bring to a boil, and reduce to a simmer.

Simmer until the chickpeas are tender (about 1½ hours). Taste a few chickpeas, to make sure they are tender.

Add the diced asparagus. Cook until tender, about 20 minutes.

Stir in half of the tarragon, and all of the parsley.

Simmer a few more minutes, and remove from the heat. Discard the bay leaf.

Purée in batches. Taste and adjust seasoning, as necessary.

Sauté the reserved asparagus tips in the olive oil, over medium-high heat, with a pinch of salt until crisp tender, about 5 minutes. Add the white wine and remaining tarragon, and cook until the wine has evaporated.

To serve:

Ladle the soup into serving bowls.

Garnish with the crisp asparagus tips.

Wine: A dry Prosécco from Treviso, with aromas of citrus, almonds and white flowers
Beer: A Belgian-style witbier, like the tart and yeasty, Cinder Block Weathered Wit

FAIRYTALE PUMPKIN
HUBBELL & HUDSON

Chef Austin Simmons is a kitchen wizard. His take on local/sustainable cuisine results in artful, sophisticated dishes that leave us blissful. This seasonal soup is the freshest take ever on pumpkin, and the drizzled brown butter garnish takes it over the top.

Recipe Notes: Enjoy the bountiful selection of fall pumpkins, and don't be intimidated about roasting them. If the contents of your raw pumpkin are liquid, it means it's not good and you should get another one. Instructions for toasting pumpkin seeds and browning butter are on page 131.

YIELD: 8 SERVINGS

6 oz	unsalted butter
⅓ cup	shallots, sliced
½ Tbsp	garlic, minced
2	thyme sprigs
1 Tbsp	salt
1 tsp	white pepper
3 lb	Fairytale pumpkin, peeled, seeded, diced
3½ cups	chicken stock
	brown butter, *for garnish*
	pumpkin seeds, toasted, *for garnish*
	chervil leaves, *for garnish*

Melt 3 ounces of butter in a large 1½ gallon pot, over medium-low heat.

Add the shallots, garlic, thyme (tied in a cheesecloth sachet), salt and pepper.

Sweat the vegetables for 10 to 15 minutes. DO NOT CARAMELIZE.

Shallots should be translucent, but still have a little crunch.

Add the pumpkin, and mix well. Add the stock, and bring up to a simmer.

Simmer until the pumpkin is fully cooked, about 30 to 45 minutes.

Remove the thyme, transfer the mixture to a blender, and process, in batches.

Add the remaining butter, in portions, to the soup, while blending.

To serve:

Ladle the soup into bowls.

Garnish with brown butter, toasted pumpkins seeds and chervil leaves.

Wine: A sparkling Grüner Veltliner Brut, with citrus aromas and peppery notes
Beer: A dark Belgian ale, like Gulden Draak Ale

SALSIFY BISQUE
QUATTRO, FOUR SEASONS HOTEL

The revamped and revitalized Four Seasons Hotel Houston debuted in 2017 — with a massive multi-million dollar renovation including a state-of-the-art Spa & Fitness Center and a new bourbon bar, Bayou & Bottle. The hotel's acclaimed restaurant Quattro remains intact as the home of the city's best brunch alongside its signature authentic Italian cuisine.

We love it when chefs turn us on to obscure ingredients, like Chef Maurizio did here. Salsify is a root vegetable, shaped like a carrot. It is also known as the oyster plant because of its oystery taste when cooked.

YIELD: 6 SERVINGS

2 lb	salsify
2 cups	extra-virgin olive oil
½	thyme bunch
½ cup	shallots, chopped
⅓ cup	leeks, chopped
⅓ cup	yellow onions, chopped
⅓ cup	celery, chopped
½ lb	parsnips
1 tsp	salt
½ tsp	white pepper
3 cups	water
1 cup	oyster mushrooms, raw, sliced
1 Tbsp	shallots, chopped
1 tsp	thyme leaves
½ cup	Madeira wine

Peel the salsify and soak them in water, to prevent oxidation.

Cut the salsify in batons (matchsticks that are about ½-inch by ½-inch and 3- to 4-inches long).

Set aside about 6 of the batons for garnish (keep them in water).

Add 1 cup of olive oil to a stockpot over medium heat.

Add the salsify and the thyme sprigs, and sauté for about 7 to 8 minutes (no color needed on the salsify).

Add the shallots, leeks, onions, celery and parsnip, salt and white pepper.

Reduce the heat to medium-low, and sweat the vegetables for about 10 to 15 minutes.

Add 3 cups of water, bring to a boil, and simmer for about 10 minutes.

Purée the vegetable mixture in the blender, adding about a ¼ cup of the remaining olive oil.

Press the mixture through a sieve.

Heat the remaining olive in a skillet, over medium-high heat. Add the mushrooms, the additional shallots and thyme leaves, and sauté for about 4 to 6 minutes.

Add the wine to deglaze the pan, and cook down for a few minutes.

Add the salsify batons, and sauté for a few minutes longer.

To serve:

Place a spoonful of the mushroom mixture and a salsify baton, in the middle of serving bowls.

Pour the soup in around it.

Wine: A crisp, Italian Pinot Grigio, with flavors of pear and citrus
Beer: A traditional German pilsner, the slightly hoppy, Weihenstephaner Pils

CREMA DE CALÇOT
BCN TASTE & TRADITION

Chef Luis Roger and front-of-the-house veteran Paco Calzo have created a dining experience unique for Houston, featuring the chef's focus on modern Spanish cuisine, alongside stellar service. Chef Luis is an El Bulli alum, passionate about technique and tradition, with a direct approach to flavors. We heart roasted leeks, and the fantastic romesco sauce is worth making on its own, as a wonderful dip for crudités, or with grilled bread.

YIELD: 6 SERVINGS

For the soup:

Grill the leeks over a medium-high open flame, for 6 to 8 minutes. At this point, the outside of the leeks will be charred black.

Remove and discard about ¾ of the burnt, crisp outer layer, then rest the remaining leeks in olive oil for an hour, to infuse the flavor (at room temperature).

Set aside around ¼ cup of this infused olive oil, to garnish the dish later.

Chop up the cooked leeks. Add the leeks to the olive oil, in a large stockpot, and simmer for 15 minutes, or until they begin to golden.

Add the potatoes and the salt. Stir, then add the water. Boil for 20 minutes, and remove from the heat.

Rest for 1 hour, with the lid on. Blend, strain, and add salt, to taste.

For the romesco sauce:

Remove the stems, membranes and seeds from the ancho chiles. Put the chiles in a bowl, and pour hot water over them. Cover, and let rehydrate for 45 minutes to an hour, then strain.

Heat the oven to 350˚F. Roast the tomatoes and garlic on a sheet pan, for about 35 minutes. When cool, squeeze the garlic out of the skins. Set aside.

Dice the bread and place on a sheet pan. Spritz with some olive oil, and toast in a 350˚F oven, for about 10 minutes, until crisp.

Boil 4 to 5 inches of water in a small saucepan, and add the almonds for 30 seconds. Strain and wrap the almonds in a towel for a minute. Slide the skins off and set aside.

Toast the almonds and hazelnuts in the 350˚F oven for about 10 minutes. Remove from the oven and wrap the hazelnuts in a towel for a minute, then remove their skins, and set aside.

Add all of the ingredients to a blender, and purée until smooth. Add salt and pepper, to taste.

To serve:

Ladle the soup into serving bowls.

Garnish with a drizzle of the leek-infused olive oil, black pepper, and grilled bread with romesco and chives.

SOUP

5	leeks
1 cup	extra-virgin olive oil
1⅛ lb	Yukon gold potato, peeled, quartered
6⅓ cups	bottled water
¾ tsp	sea salt

ROMESCO SAUCE
Yield: 2 cups

3	ancho chiles, dried
2 cups	hot water
2¾ cups	Roma tomato
¾ cup	garlic cloves, unpeeled
3½ oz	rustic country bread
⅓ cup	almonds, raw
⅓ cup	hazelnuts
⅓ cup	extra-virgin olive oil
1 Tbsp	sherry vinegar
to taste	salt and pepper

leek-infused olive oil, *for garnish*
black pepper, freshly ground, *for garnish*
chives, minced, *for garnish*
grilled bread

Wine: A Spanish Godello
Beer: A Belgian witbier, like Estrella Damm Inedit

THIRD COAST SEAFOOD STEW
AGAVE RIO

3	New Mexico chiles, dried
3	guajillo chiles, dried
STOCK	
1	ginger root (4-inch)
18	Gulf shrimp (16/20s)
2 Tbsp	olive oil
1 cup	yellow onion, chopped
1	carrot, rough chopped
3	celery stalks, chopped
1	lemongrass stalk (3-inch), white part only
5	peppercorns
4	thyme sprigs
2	bay leaves, bruised
2	oregano sprigs
6	gumbo crab shells
6 cups	water
STEW	
2½ Tbsp	extra-virgin olive oil
10	Roma tomatoes, chopped
2	red bell peppers, seeded, chopped
8	garlic cloves, rough chopped
1 cup	red onion, chopped
1	chipotle, in adobo sauce
1 Tbsp	oregano leaves
1 Tbsp	thyme leaves
1	jalapeño, seeded, chopped
1 tsp	ginger, small dice
1½ cups	dry white wine
1 lb	snapper, cubed
24	crab claws
1 Tbsp	sherry vinegar
1 Tbsp	lime juice
PESTO	
1	cilantro bunch
½ cup	cotija
3 Tbsp	pumpkin seeds, toasted
2	garlic cloves, peeled
¼ cup	olive oil
to taste	salt and pepper

Eric Aldis is one busy and super-talented chef. Agave Rio is a gorgeous restaurant and event space in Katy. They serve up big flavors, like this fantastic soup, featuring the freshest seafood. The aromatics while you're making it are incredible, and the pesto can be used in a variety of ways beyond the soup.

Recipe Notes: You may purchase gumbo crab shells from a fish monger, like Airline Seafood or Blue Horizon Seafood. Instructions for toasting pumpkin seeds are on page 131.

YIELD: 6 SERVINGS

Remove the stems, seeds and membranes of the chiles and rehydrate in a bowl of hot water, covered, for 30 minutes.

For the stock:

Peel the ginger, and char over an open flame, for about 5 minutes. Set aside.

Peel and devein the shrimp, leaving the tails on, reserving the shells for the stock, and the shrimp for the stew.

Heat the olive oil in a stockpot, over medium heat. Add the onion, carrot and celery, lemongrass and ginger. Stir to combine. Add the peppercorns, thyme, bay leaves and oregano and cook until the vegetables are soft and the onion is translucent, about 15 minutes.

Add the shrimp shells and the crab shells. Add the water, bring to a boil, and let cook on medium-high for 1 hour.

For the stew:

Heat the olive oil in a deep stockpot, over medium-high heat. Add the tomatoes, peppers, garlic, onion, chipotle, herbs, jalapeños and ginger.

Drain the soaking chiles, and add them to the stockpot. Stir the mixture, and continue cooking, for about 10 minutes.

Add the white wine, and increase the heat to high. Bring to a boil, and reduce to a simmer, for about 30 minutes.

Add the vegetable mixture to a blender, in batches and purée for 6 minutes, returning the purée to the stockpot, through a strainer. Stir to combine, over medium heat.

Add the fish and shrimp, and cook for 5 minutes. Add the crab claws, and cook for about 45 seconds longer.

Turn off the heat. Stir in the sherry vinegar and the lime juice.

For the pesto:

Combine all the ingredients in a blender, and process until smooth. Add salt and pepper, to taste.

To serve:

Ladle the stew into serving bowls.
Add a tablespoon of pesto, and garnish with parsley, green onions, cotija and pumpkin seeds, if desired.

Wine: A Mosel river, German Riesling, like the ones from the legendary J.J. Prum
Beer: A malty American brown ale, like Dogfish Head Palo Santo Marron

MILO HAMILTON'S PASTA E FAGIOLI
DAMIAN'S CUCINA ITALIANA

Pasta e Fagioli has been on the menu at Damian's for over 20 years. It was renamed after Milo Hamilton, "the voice of the Astros," once he professed his love for the dish, and sent so many folks to the restaurant to try it. The story goes that he would order one vodka martini and one bowl of his beloved soup, each and every time he came in.

A traditional Italian dish, pasta e fagioli, means "pasta and beans" and was typically considered a peasant dish, as it's made of fairly inexpensive ingredients.

YIELD: 8 SERVINGS

In a medium-sized braising pan, sauté the pancetta in the olive oil, over a medium flame, until the pancetta is almost brown.

Add the onion, celery, garlic and parsley, and sauté until the vegetables are soft, about 10 minutes.

Add the basil, and tomatoes with their juice, and cook a couple of minutes longer.

Add the chicken stock and chicken base, and bring to a boil.

Drop in the potatoes, salt, black pepper, red pepper and oregano.

Boil for about 10 minutes, or until the potatoes are tender.

Add the beans along with their juice, and return to a boil (beans are already cooked).

Remove from the heat.

Fill a stockpot with 6 cups of water, and bring to a boil.

Add the pasta, and cook until al dente.

To serve:

Add a few spoonfuls of cooked pasta to serving bowls.

Top with the bean soup.

Garnish with parsley leaves.

2 Tbsp	olive oil
6 oz	pancetta, ¼-inch dice
¾ cup	yellow onion, finely diced
¾ cup	celery, finely chopped
2½ Tbsp	garlic cloves, peeled, finely chopped
2 Tbsp	Italian parsley, chopped
2 Tbsp	basil, chopped
½ cup	crushed tomatoes, with juice
3 cups	chicken stock
¼ Tbsp	chicken base
1 lb	potatoes, peeled, ¼-inch dice
½ Tbsp	salt
½ Tbsp	black pepper
1 tsp	red pepper, crushed
1⅛ Tbsp	dry oregano
3 cans	cannellini beans (19-oz)
6 cups	water
½ cup	Ditalini rigati pasta, dry
	parsley leaves, *for garnish*

Wine: An Barbera d'Alba, with high acid, and low tannins
Beer: An imperial pilsner, like Dogfish Head My Antonia

THREE MELON
CARACOL

Chef Ruben Ortega's desserts are legendary, and the dining room at Caracol is a stunning setting in which to enjoy them. This versatile soup can be drizzled with a little gin or tequila for a savory appetizer, served as a palate cleanser, or as the finale to dinner, and strikes just the right balance between tangy and sweet. It's fresh and fun!

Recipe Notes: Depending on how sweet/ripe your fruit is, you may need to add more, or less simple syrup.

YIELD: 4 TO 6 SERVINGS

CANTALOUPE GRANITA

¾ cup	granulated sugar
¾ cup	water
1	cantaloupe

MELON SOUP

1	honeydew melon
½ tsp	xanthan gum
2 Tbsp	sugar

WATERMELON SORBET

½ cup	simple syrup
4 cups	watermelon, rind removed, seeded, cubed
1 Tbsp	lime juice

lime zest, *for garnish*
micro-mint leaves, *for garnish*
melon, small dice, *for garnish*

For the cantaloupe granita:

Combine the water and sugar, in a medium saucepan. Stir over medium heat, until the sugar dissolves. Increase the heat, and bring to a boil. Reduce the heat to medium, and simmer for about 3 minutes. Transfer the syrup to a bowl, and chill thoroughly.

Peel and seed the cantaloupe, and cut into pieces, reserving ¼ cup for the garnish (to be small diced).

Purée the fruit in a blender, until liquefied. Add ⅓ cup of the syrup to the puréed fruit, and mix well. (Reserve the rest of the syrup for the sorbet)

Pour the cantaloupe mixture into a prechilled glass loaf pan. Place it uncovered, into the freezer.

Scrape with a fork every ½ hour, until almost completely frozen but still grainy, about 3 to 4 hours.

For the melon soup:

Peel and seed the honeydew, and cut into pieces, reserving a ¼ cup (to be small diced) for the garnish. Juice enough of the honeydew to yield 4 cups of juice, and chill in the refrigerator.

Mix the xanthan gum into one tablespoon of water. When the soup is chilled, add the xanthan gum and the sugar. Mix well, in a blender, or with a hand blender, until incorporated. Refrigerate until needed.

For the watermelon sorbet:

Peel and seed the watermelon, and cut into cubes. Reserve a ¼ cup of the watermelon (to be small diced), for the garnish. Purée the watermelon cubes in a blender. Using a fine mesh strainer or sieve, pour and press the blended mixture through, to remove the seeds and any extra pulp. Stir into the chilled simple syrup and lime juice. Freeze in an ice cream maker and process until it has a soft-serve texture. Serve right away or place into an air-tight container and freeze for 2 hours, until firm.

To serve:

Place a few tablespoons of granita in the center of the bowl. Pour about a half cup of honeydew soup around the granita. Put a quenelle (*football-shaped scoop*) of watermelon sorbet on top of the granita. Garnish with the lime zest, micro-mint leaves and the melon.

Wine: A Moscato d'Asti
Beer: A spicy IPA, like No Label What the Hatch Chile IPA

MINTED KIWI
JODYCAKES

We are big fans of Jodycakes - an incredibly talented pastry-chef who creates dazzling desserts utilizing the freshest ingredients and local sourcing, with a variety of options, including organic and vegan, along with dairy, egg and gluten-free variations, as desired. In other words, she's singing our song (plus she's one cool chick).

Recipe Notes: You may substitute apricot or real apple juice for the peach nectar. You may also garnish with mint sprigs or leaves.

YIELD: 4 TO 6 SERVINGS

Cut both ends off of the kiwis.

Slide a spoon (I like using a grapefruit spoon, with a serrated tip) in between the skin and the fruit. Scoop out the flesh in a circular motion, trying to stay as close to the skin as possible.

Add the peeled kiwis to a blender, along with the mint, yogurt, cream, vinegar, sugar and nectar.

Blend until smooth (seeds will remain whole).

In a separate chilled bowl, beat the cream and sugar into soft peaks, by hand, or with a mixer.

Fold the cream into the kiwi mixture, until combined.

Place in the refrigerator to chill, for at least 2 hours.

To serve:

Pour the soup into coupes, martini glasses or small cups.

Garnish with kiwi wheels.

3	kiwis, large
6	mint leaves
1 cup	plain Greek yogurt
1/3 cup	heavy cream
1½ Tbsp	apple cider vinegar
½ cup	granulated sugar
1/3 cup	peach nectar
½ cup	heavy cream
2 Tbsp	granulated sugar
	kiwi wheels, *for garnish*

Wine: An Austrian Trockenbeerenauslese, showcasing intense sweet fruit and vibrant acidity

Beer: A dry-hopped farmhouse ale, like Prairie 'Ace', from Prairie Artisan Ales

CHOCOLATE A L'ORANGE
DESSERT GALLERY BAKERY & CAFÉ

Sara Brook is a Houston legend - celebrating her 20th year in business! Jodie has been a devoted customer since day one. Sweet Sara shared her delicious carrot cake and white chocolate macadamia nut cookie recipes for my "Houston Classic Desserts" and "Houston Small Plates & Sips" cookbooks. This is a fun recipe, and we love orange flavor with chocolate. My sweet 8-year-old cousin, Olivia, aced this recipe, with ease!

Recipe Notes: Variation options: substitute raspberries and raspberry liqueur, for the orange zest and Grand Marnier. Substitute vanilla or Kahlua, for the Grand Marnier.

YIELD: 6 SERVINGS

For the soup:

Combine the orange zest, milk and half-and-half in a pot over medium heat.

Bring to a simmer (not a full boil). Remove from the heat, and cover.

Let the mixture stand until the liquid is infused with the orange flavor, about 25 minutes.

Return the pan to the heat. Simmer (do not boil). Add the chocolate, and whisk until melted.

In a small bowl, whisk the egg yolks.

Continue whisking the yolks, while adding some of the hot chocolate liquid. Slowly pour the egg and chocolate mixture into the pot, with the rest of the chocolate liquid.

Add the salt and Grand Marnier. Continue whisking, until slightly thickened.

For the croutons:

Preheat oven to 350˚F.

Combine the cinnamon and sugar.

Toss the cubed croissants or bread with butter, and then into the cinnamon and sugar.

Arrange the bread on a baking sheet, and toast until golden brown.

For the whipped cream:

Add the heavy cream and the Grand Marnier, to a chilled bowl.

Beat until stiff peaks form.

To serve:

Ladle the soup into serving bowls (be sure to serve warm).

Top with a dollop of whipped cream and croutons.

Garnish with orange zest, if desired.

SOUP

½ tsp	orange zest
2½ cups	milk
2½ cups	half-and-half
1 lb	semi-sweet chocolate, finely chopped
2	egg yolks
¼ tsp	salt
2 tsp	Grand Marnier

CROUTONS

1 Tbsp	sugar
½ tsp	cinnamon
2	croissants or rolls, cubed
2 oz	unsalted butter, melted

WHIPPED CREAM

1 cup	heavy cream, chilled
2 tsp	Grand Marnier
	orange zest, *for garnish*

Wine: A Recioto della Valpolicella, from Veneto, Italy
Beer: A stout, like Southern Star Buried Hatchet Stout

SWEETNESS OF LIFE
DEER LAKE LODGE

We are so inspired by the mission at the magnificent 50-acre, eco-friendly Deer Lake Lodge and Health Spa in Montgomery – just minutes from The Woodlands.

They help crazy-busy folks like us, tap into a slower, healthier way of living. Offerings include excellent yoga classes and a very cool cleansing program, as well as other services, to bring the body back into balance.

This detoxifying soup is screaming fresh, and reminds us why we've become so passionate about beautiful, organic ingredients and their potential healing properties.

Recipe Notes: Make sure you use high quality, organic essential oils. Real Salt is a brand unrefined sea salt, full of natural minerals.

YIELD: 2 SERVINGS

Process the carrots, kale, celery, lemon and ginger root through a juicer.

Add the juices, ginger oil, lemon oil, avocado, cumin and salt to a blender.

Blend until well combined and serve.

To serve:

Pour the soup into small bowls.

Garnish with parsley leaves.

10	carrots, organic
1	kale, organic, handful
2	celery stalks, organic
1	lemon, organic
1	ginger root, (thumb-sized)
1 drop	ginger essential oil
1 drop	lemon essential oil
1	avocado
1 tsp	ground cumin
½ tsp	Real Salt
	parsley leaves, *for garnish*

AVOCADO DETOX
ALI MILLER, R.D.

We met Ali Miller, R.D. when Jodie served as editor, and Erin helped print her fabulous cookbook, "Naturally Nourished: Food-As-Medicine For Optimal Health." We are big followers, and have learned so much from Ali. This recipe is a great intro to her 10-Day Real Food Detox program, which is available online, and recommended quarterly.

Recipe Notes: For a little crunch, use the remaining cucumber as a garnish. You can also top with kale chips!

YIELD: 2 SERVINGS

Peel and seed the cucumber and avocado.

Add the cucumber, avocado, onion, garlic, lemon or lime juice, vinegar, cilantro and water to a blender (Vitamix is the best!).

Purée on high until smooth. Blend in the salt, chili powder and the remaining ingredients.

Be sure to have the blender running, while adding the olive oil, to best emulsify the soup.

To serve:

Pour the soup into small bowls.

Garnish with tomato, parsley and smoked paprika.

½	cucumber
½	avocado
1 Tbsp	onion, minced
1	garlic clove
1 Tbsp	lemon or lime juice
1 Tbsp	apple cider vinegar
⅓ cup	cilantro
½ cup	filtered water
¼ tsp	sea salt (Celtic)
¼ tsp	chili powder
dash	cayenne pepper
1½ tsp	extra-virgin olive oil

tomato, diced,
for garnish
parsley leaves,
for garnish
smoked paprika,
for garnish

Most stocks can be refrigerated for 2 to 3 days. Frozen stock will keep for several months. It is super important to let the stock (and all soup), cool properly before storing in the refrigerator. They will become a breeding ground of bacteria, if refrigerated immediately.

Vegetable Stock

Yield: 3 quarts

14 cups	water
4	carrots (medium), sliced in 2-inch pieces
4	celery stalks, large dice
1	onion (medium), large dice
1	garlic head, cut in half
1	parsley stems, bunch
3	bay leaves
1	thyme bunch
1 tsp	peppercorns, whole
1 tsp	allspice, whole

Combine all of the ingredients in a large stockpot. Bring to a boil, and then lower heat to maintain a low simmer. Cook until reduced, about 1½ to 2 hours.

Remove from the heat and strain through a fine sieve. Let the stock cool before refrigerating.

Chicken Stock

Yield: 3 quarts

3 lb	chicken bones
2	Spanish onions (large), quartered, skin on
4	celery stalks, chopped, leaves on
2	leeks, white, light green parts only, split, washed
2	carrots (large), chopped
2 Tbsp	olive oil
2	bay leaves
8	thyme sprigs
10	whole black peppercorns
1 gal	water

Heat the oven to 425°F.

Place the bones, onions, celery, leeks and carrots on a sheet pan, and toss with the olive oil. Roast until the bones and vegetables are golden brown, for about 30 to 45 minutes.

Transfer all to a large stockpot. Add the remaining ingredients, and bring to a boil. Reduce the heat to a simmer, and cook for 3 to 4 hours. Be sure to skim the impurities that rise to the top every half hour or so. Remove from the heat and strain. Let the stock cool before refrigerating.

Beef Broth

Yield: 3 quarts

5 lb	meaty beef bones
2	onions, peeled, halved
3	carrots, peeled, chopped
2	celery stalks, chopped
1 gal	water
6	parsley sprigs
6	thyme sprigs
1 tsp	salt
1 tsp	black peppercorns, cracked

Heat the oven to 425°F.

Place the bones on a sheet pan, and roast them for 30 to 40 minutes, turning them once.

Transfer the bones to a large pot. Add the onions, carrots, celery and the water (or enough water to cover the contents by at least an inch or two). Bring to a boil, then reduce to a simmer. Skim off all the impurities that rise to the top. When the foam ceases, add the parsley, thyme, salt and pepper.

Simmer for about 3 hours. Strain the stock through a cheese cloth-lined colander or strainer. Let the stock cool before refrigerating.

Duck Stock

Yield: 3½ quarts

1	duck carcass or 2 pounds duck bones
1 cup	onion, chopped
½ cup	carrot, chopped
½ cup	celery, chopped

1	red chile, slit lengthwise
4	garlic cloves, crushed
¼ cup	ginger, sliced, crushed
2	star anise
4	cilantro sprigs
6	thyme sprigs
2	bay leaves
½ tsp	black peppercorns, lightly crushed
1 gal	water

Place everything into a large stockpot and cover with water. Bring to a boil then reduce to a simmer and cook for 2 hours, partially covered, skimming any scum that rises to the top.

After simmering, strain into a bowl, pressing the bones and vegetables to gently to remove all the liquid. Discard all solids. Let the stock cool before refrigerating.

Seafood Stock

Yield: 2 quarts

2 lb	fish heads (gills removed), or a combination of shrimp, crab or lobster shells, cleaned
2	onions (medium), quartered
2	carrots, rough chopped
2	celery stalks, with leaves, rough chopped
2	bay leaves
8	peppercorns, lightly cracked
4	thyme sprigs, tied together
½ cup	dry white wine

Combine all of the ingredients in a stockpot, cover with water. Bring to a boil, and reduce to a simmer. Skim any impurities/foam that rises to the top. Let simmer for about an hour. Let the stock cool, before straining through a cheese cloth-lined colander or strainer. This will only keep for a few days in the refrigerator; it will keep for several months in the freezer.

Mimi's Split End Chicken & Dumplings
Nelda Hicks

Yield: 10 to 12 servings

4 lb	chicken, whole
to taste	salt and pepper
2½ cups	all-purpose flour
1 tsp	baking powder
1 Tbsp	shortening
3	eggs
½ cup	milk
1 cup	heavy cream

Season the chicken with salt and pepper. Add to a large stock pot, and cover with water.

Boil until tender. Remove the chicken, cool and debone. Save the broth.

Sift the flour and baking powder together, and cut in the shortening. Beat the eggs, until mixed. Add the milk, and pour into the flour mixture.

Mix with a fork, until it mounds up. Divide the dough into 6 portions, then roll each portion on a floured board, until paper thin.

Cut into strips or 1½-inch diamonds, and place on floured tray. Bring the broth to a boil; drop the dumplings into the broth, one at a time.

When all dumplings have been added to the broth, then add 1 cup cream. Mix well. Put the chicken back into the pot, on top of the dumplings. Spoon some broth over the chicken, to keep it moist. Cover the pot, and keep warm until serving.

Pickled Onions

Yield: about 2 cups

1	red onion (medium), thinly sliced
¾-1 cup	apple cider or red wine vinegar
½ tsp	salt
1 tsp	honey or sugar

Bring the onion, vinegar, salt, and honey (or sugar) to a boil in a saucepan, over medium-high heat. Remove from heat, and allow mixture to steep until the onion is tender, about 20 minutes. Cool completely before serving

Toasted Pumpkin Seeds (Pepitas)

Yield: 1 cup

1 cup	raw pumpkin seeds
1 Tbsp	unsalted butter or olive oil
1 tsp	salt

Heat the oven to 300°F

Spread the seeds on a sheet pan. Drizzle with butter (or olive oil) and sprinkle with salt. Bake for 30 to 40 minutes, stirring frequently, until golden brown.

To brown butter:

Melt unsalted butter in a small sauce pan, over medium heat. Swirl the pan a few times to ensure butter is cooking evenly. It will begin to foam, and the foam will turn golden - once you smell the nutty aroma, pull the pan off the heat. Strain into a heat-proof bowl, leaving behind as much of the sediment as possible.

To clarify butter:

Melt unsalted butter in a saucepan, over low heat. Let it simmer until the all of the foam has risen to the top. Remove from the heat. Skim off the white foam layer. Pour the butter through a cheesecloth-lined strainer in a glass storage container.

RESTAURANT LISTINGS

51fifteen Cuisine and Cocktails
5175 Westheimer Rd
Houston, TX 77056
(713) 963-8067
www.51fifteen.com

Agave Rio
1138 Farm To Market 1463
Katy, TX 77494
(281) 665-3337
www.agaverio.com

Ali Miller, R.D.
701 Richmond Ave
Houston, TX 77006
(832) 559-0155
www.alimillerrd.com

Andes Café
2311 Canal St
Houston, TX 77003
(832) 659-0063
www.andescafé.com

Ara
Royal Sonesta Hotel
2222 West Loop South
Houston, TX 77027
(713) 627-7600
www.sonesta.com/RoyalHouston

Arthur Ave
1111 Studewood St
Houston, TX 77008
(832) 582-7146
www.arthuravehou.com

BCN Taste & Tradition
4210 Roseland St
Houston, TX 77006
(832) 834-3411
www.bcnhouston.com

Bernadine's
1801 N Shepherd Dr
Houston, TX 77008
(713) 864-2565
www.treadsack.com/bernadines

Boada Cuisine
6510 Del Monte Dr
Houston, TX 77057
(713) 782-3011
www.boadacuisine.com

Borgo Food Station
3641 West Alabama St
Houston, TX 77027
(832) 940-2126
www.borgofoodstation.com

Brasserie 19
1962 West Gray St
Houston, TX 77019
(713) 524-1919
www.brasserie19.com

Cafe Annie
1800 Post Oak Blvd
Houston, TX 77056
(713) 840-1111
www.caféanniehouston.com

Caracol
2200 Post Oak Blvd
Houston, TX 77056
(713) 622-9996
www.caracol.net

The Original Carrabba's - Kirby
3115 Kirby
Houston, TX 77098
(713) 522-3131

Carrabba's - Voss
1399 South Voss
Houston, TX 77057
(713) 468-0868
www.carrabbasoriginal.com

Ciao Bello
5161 San Felipe St
Houston, TX 77056
(713) 960-0333
www.ciaobellohouston.com

Damian's Cucina Italiana
3011 Smith St
Houston, TX 77006
(713) 522-0439
www.damians.com

Deer Lake Lodge
10500 Deer Lake Lodge Rd
Montgomery, TX 77316
(936) 647-1383
www.deerlakelodge.com

Dessert Gallery Bakery & Café
3600 Kirby Dr, Ste. D
Houston, TX 77098
(713) 522-9999
www.dessertgallery.com

Eculent
709 Harris Ave
Kemah, TX 77565
(713) 429-4311
www.eculent.com

Chef Erin Smith Feges
esmith44@msn.com
Twitter - @PurslaneErin
Instagram - @purslane_erin

Foreign Correspondents
4721 N Main St, Ste. A
Houston, TX 77009
(713) 864-8424
www.treadsack.com/foreigncorrespondents

Giacomo's Cibo e Vino
3215 Westheimer Rd
Houston, TX 77098
(713) 522-1934
www.giacomosciboevino.com

Good Dog - Heights
903 Studewood St
Houston, TX 77008
(832) 800-3647

Good Dog - Montrose
1312 West Alabama
Houston, TX 77006
(346) 800-3647
www.gooddoghouston.com

Grace's
3111 Kirby Dr
Houston, TX 77098
(713) 728-6410
www.gracesonkirby.com

Harold's Tap Room
350 W 19th St
Houston, TX 77008
(713) 360-6204
www.haroldsheights.com/tap-room

Helen Greek Food and Wine
2429 Rice Blvd
Houston, TX 77005
(832) 831-7133
www.helengreekfoodandwine.com

Himalaya
6652 Southwest Fwy
Houston, TX 77074
(713) 532-2837
www.himalayarestauranthouston.com

Hubbell & Hudson
24 Waterway Ave, Ste. 125
The Woodlands, TX 77380
(281) 203-5600
www.hubbellandhudson.com

Hungry's Café - West University
2356 Rice Blvd
Houston, TX 77005
(713) 523-8652

Hungry's Café - Energy Corridor
14714 Memorial Dr
Houston, TX 77079
(281) 493-1520
www.hungryscafé.com

Ibiza Food & Wine Bar
2450 Louisiana St
Houston, TX 77006
(713) 524-0004
www.ibizafoodandwinebar.com

Izakaya
318 Gray St
Houston, TX 77002
(713) 527-8988
www.houstonizakaya.com

Jodycakes
Custom Orders Only
(832) 722-4123
www.jodycakes.com

Jonathan's The Rub
9061 Gaylord St
Houston, TX 77024
(713) 465-8200
www.jonathanstherub.com

RESTAURANT LISTINGS

Kenny & Ziggy's - Galleria/Uptown
2327 Post Oak Blvd
Houston, TX 77056
(713) 871-8883

Kenny & Ziggy's - West University
5172 Buffalo Speedway
Houston, TX 77005
(832) 767-1136
www.kennyandziggys.com

Killen's BBQ
3613 Broadway St
Pearland, TX 77581-4201
(281) 485-2272
www.killensbarbecue.com

Liberty Kitchen and Oysterette
4224 San Felipe St
Houston, Texas 77027
713-622-1010
http://www.libertykitchenoysterette.com

Local Foods - West University
2424 Dunstan Rd
Houston, TX 77005
713) 521-7800

Local Foods - River Oaks
2555 Kirby Dr
Houston, TX 77019
(713) 255-4440

Local Foods - Tanglewood
5740 San Felipe St
Houston, TX 77057
(713) 789-0642
www.houstonlocalfoods.com

Main Kitchen 806 Lounge at the JW
Marriott Downtown
806 Main St
Houston, TX 77002
(713) 400-1293
www.jwmarriotthotelhouston.com/
   mainkitchen

Manor House, Houstonian Hotel,
Club & Spa
111 N Post Oak Ln
Houston, TX 77024
(713) 685-6840
www.houstonian.com/ManorHouse.aspx

Ninfa's on Navigation
2704 Navigation Blvd
Houston, TX 77003
(713) 228-1175
www.ninfas.com

Oporto Fooding House & Wine
125 West Gray
Houston, TX 77019
(713) 528-0115
www.oportomidtown.us

Oxheart
1302 Nance St
Houston, TX 77002
(832) 830-8592
www.oxhearthouston.com

Palm (The) Restaurant
6100 Westheimer Rd
Houston, TX 77057
(713) 977-2544
www.thepalm.com/Houston

Pax Americana
4319 Montrose Blvd
Houston, TX 77006
(713) 239-0228
www.paxamericanahtx.com

Peska Seafood Culture
1700 Post Oak Blvd, Ste. 190
Houston, TX 77056
(713) 961-9229
www.peska.us

Peli Peli -The Galleria
5085 Westheimer Rd
Houston, TX 77056
(281) 257-9500

Peli Peli - Vintage Park
110 Vintage Park Blvd
Houston, TX 77070
(281) 257-9500
www.pelipeli.com

Prohibition Supperclub & Bar
1008 Prairie St
Houston, TX 77002
(281) 940-4636
www.prohibitionhouston.com

Quattro, Four Seasons Hotel
1300 Lamar St
Houston, TX 77010
(713) 276-4700
www.quattrorestauranthouston.com

Rainbow Lodge
2011 Ella Blv
Houston, TX 77008
(713) 861-8666
www.rainbow-lodge.com

Ritual
602 Studewood St
Houston, TX 77007
(832) 203-5180
www.ritualhouston.com

Ripe Cuisine
Locations Vary —
Details on Website
(713) 876-4768
www.ripe-cuisine.com

River Oaks Country Club
(Membership Required)
1600 River Oaks Blvd
Houston, TX 77019
(713) 529-4321
www.riveroakscc.net

Roost
1972 Fairview St
Houston, TX 77019
(713) 523-7667
www.iloveroost.com

Ruggles Black
3963 Kirby Dr
Houston, TX 77098
(832) 530-4493
www.rugglesblack.com

Ruggles Green - Memorial
801 Town And Country Blvd
Houston, TX 77024
(713) 464-5557

Ruggles Green - The Heights
748 E 11th St
Houston, TX 77008
(713) 714-8460

Ruggles Green - Upper Kirby
2305 West Alabama
Houston, TX 77098
(713) 533-0777

Ruggles Green - Sugarland
15903 City Walk
Sugar Land, TX 77479
(281) 565-1175
www.rugglesgreen.com

Chef Alvin Schultz
Private Dining - Underground
Dinners - Location Varies
www.eatdrinkexperience.com

Songkran Thai Kitchen - Uptown Park
1101-08 Uptown Park Blvd
Houston, TX 77056
(713) 993-9096

Songkran Thai Grill - Sugarland
2258 Texas Dr
Sugar Land, TX 77479
(281) 670-8525
www.songkranthaikitchen.com

State of Grace
3258 Westheimer Rd
Houston, TX 77098
(832) 942-5080
www.stateofgracetx.com

Table 57 Dining & Drinks - HEB
5895 San Felipe
Houston, TX 77057
(713) 978-5860
https://www.heb.com/static-page/
        Table-57-Dining-and-Drinks

Tony's
3755 Richmond Ave
Houston, TX 77046
(713) 622-6778
www.tonyshouston.com

INDEX

INDEX

NOTES

ACKNOWLEDGMENT

As always, a HUGE thanks to all the chefs that are gracious enough to share their recipes. I'm such an incredibly fortunate girl that Houston has become such a delicious culinary mecca!

These books have truly enriched my life. Although I get paid mostly 'in flavor', the relationships I have developed with many of these chefs and restaurateurs, are priceless. As I am a former restaurteur-turned designer-turned cookbook author/food-wine writer, I truly love my many occupations, and my restaurant 'families,' that I have picked up along the way. I am indeed blessed, but my waistline, not so much! Ha.

I have such wonderful childhood memories of my grandmother, Mimi, making chicken & dumplings and seafood gumbo, at Crystal beach. I honestly got a little choked up several times, working on this book. I lost my Mimi about a year into this project, but have tried to channel her daily, when recipe testing.

My sister-from-another-mister, Jodie Eisenhardt, is my partner in culinary crime and I would not be near as fat, or happy, without her in my life. She is an amazing writer, cook and recipe tester-extraordinaire; she is much appreciated. It was a lot of fun to not the be in crazy-cookbook mode alone, on this one.

I must always thank the incomparable Kit Wohl, who not only led me down this path, but continues to support me in all my endeavors. I am beyond blessed to have her in my life. I must also thank my ex-husband, Billy, whose help is always appreciated. He did erase two edited versions of my last book (on accident, lol), but he has shared his many talents over the years, and has taught me much.

Pairing assistance was immense: Shepard Ross went above and beyond, on this one. Thanks to all the featured sommeliers, cicerones and chefs for their assistance, and also to Janiz Frago, Guy Stout, Jeff King and Kevin Trevino.

Big thanks to Diane Hause, Jennifer Howard, Jeff Kane and Charles Flood, for their proofreading and editing skills.

Public relations folks: Paula Murphy, Katherine Orellana Ross, Kimberly Park, Dragana Harris, Kim Padgett, Stuart Rosenberg and Mark Sullivan, Nick Scurfield and Brittany Meisner— thanks for all of your help and assistance.

As always, recipe testers and tasters were plentiful: Jody Rigdon, Dragana Harris, Kim Mineo, Cathi Walsh, Patrise Shuttle-worth-Bittick, Rhonda Stone Feinberg, Leigh Pohlmeier Williams, Carrie Hardaker, Maureen Demar Hall, Kitsie Gaines Forrest, Gina Dibello Cardwell, Jennifer Howard, Kim Mineo, Ramiro Casas, Denise Hyden, Olivia Jestice, Andrea Jestice, Ronnie Flagiello, Michelle Comstock, Jonathan Beitler, April McGee, Yvette Sales and Jeanette Jenkins— thanks for your time, input and taste buds.

My dear friend Molly Modesett, gave me the gorgeous bowl on the cover, made by the fabulous William Wilhelmi, of Wilhelmi & Holland Gallery in Corpus Christi. Big thanks to Natalie Vaclavik/Victory Wine Group, Jim Veal, Heather Gorman, Kim Mineo and Katherine and Geri Drucker, who were kind enough to lend me set decorations.

As usual, any errors or omissions are purely my doing. If you have any questions or comments, find me on Facebook, Twitter @erinhickscooks, Instagram @erinhickscooks or send an email to: erin@erinhickscooks.com.

ARA, ROYAL SONESTA HOTEL • PESKA SEAFOOD CULTURE
THE RUB • BOADA CUISINE • IBIZA FOOD & WINE BAR • TAE
• ECULENT • PAX AMERICANA • MANOR HOUSE, THE HOUS
TAP ROOM • CHEF ERIN SMITH FEGES • CAFE ANNIE • RITUA
HELEN GREEK FOOD & WINE • THE ORIGINAL CARRABBA'S •
• RUGGLES BLACK • PROHIBITION SUPPERCLUB & BAR • T
MARRIOTT • GOOD DOG • LIBERTY KITCHEN & OYSTERETTE
• KENNY & ZIGGY'S • HUNGRY'S CAFÉ • BORGO FOOD STATIO
• THE ORIGINAL NINFA'S ON NAVIGATION • ROOST • RIVE
CHEF ALVIN SCHULTZ • GIACOMOS CIBO Y VINO • HUBBELL
TRADITION • AGAVE RIO • DAMIAN'S CUCINA ITALIANA • CAR
LODGE • ALI MILLER, R.D. • ARA, ROYAL SONESTA HOTEL • PE
& WINE • JONATHAN'S THE RUB • BOADA CUISINE • IBIZA F
• CHEF RONNIE KILLEN • ECULENT • PAX AMERICANA • M
MARK COX • HAROLD'S TAP ROOM • CHEF ERIN SMITH FEGE
51FIFTEEN • HIMALAYA • HELEN GREEK FOOD & WINE • THE
BERNADINE'S • GRACE'S • RUGGLES BLACK • PROHIBITION
AT THE DOWNTOWN JW MARRIOTT • GOOD DOG • LIBERTY
LOCAL FOODS • OXHEART • KENNY & ZIGGY'S • HUNGRY'S
FOREIGN CORRESPONDENTS • THE ORIGINAL NINFA'S ON N
GRACE • ARTHUR AVE • CHEF ALVIN SCHULTZ • GIACOMOS (
HOTEL • BCN TASTE & TRADITION • AGAVE RIO • DAMIAN'S C
& CAFÉ • DEER LAKE LODGE • ALI MILLER, R.D. • ARA, ROYA
OPORTO FOODING HOUSE & WINE • JONATHAN'S THE RUB •
DRINKS • RIPE CUISINE • CHEF RONNIE KILLEN • ECULENT
SPA & RESORT • CHEF MARK COX • HAROLD'S TAP ROOM •
19 • RAINBOW LODGE • 51FIFTEEN • HIMALAYA • HELEN GRE
CIAO BELLO/TONY'S • BERNADINE'S • GRACE'S • RUGGLES
KITCHEN 806 LOUNGE AT THE DOWNTOWN JW MARRIOTT • GC
KITCHEN/GRILL • LOCAL FOODS • OXHEART • KENNY & ZIGG